Wellington ~ *the dark side*

Wellington
the dark side

A location guide to murder, mayhem and nefarious activity in the capital city

William Minchin

STEELE ROBERTS
AOTEAROA NEW ZEALAND

First edition, January 2005. Please write, fax or email about other events worthy of inclusion ~
we know there are more. Contributors of stories used will get a free copy of the next edition.
Please also contact us with any corrections or additional information, which we will incorporate a.s.a.p.

National Library of New Zealand Cataloguing-in-Publication Data
Minchin, William, 1967-
Wellington, the dark side : a location guide to murder, mayhem
and nefarious activity in the capital city / William Minchin.
Includes index.
ISBN 1-877338-29-X
1. Crime scenes—New Zealand—Wellington—Guidebooks.
2. Wellington (N.Z.)—Guidebooks.
364.99363—dc 22

STEELE ROBERTS LTD
Box 9321 Wellington Aotearoa New Zealand
Fax 04 499 0056 • info@SteeleRoberts.co.nz • www.SteeleRoberts.co.nz

Contents

Evidence from the La Mattina trial (page 25): the painstakingly reassembled
murder weapons, including a teapot with a complete palm print.
Les Cleveland collection

Read on … at your peril

Beware … this is a guide to Wellington landmarks that some tourism officials would rather you didn't know about ~ murder scenes, riots, dens of ill-repute and more.

Sir Robert Jones once said that Wellington could be bracketed with Dar-Es-Salaam, Port au Prince and Nukualofa as one of the world's seedier capitals. We may not agree, but it's no South Seas paradise either. It has an underbelly that has been gathering grime for 160 years. This guide maps some of its nastiest sores ~ events, both historical and contemporary, that have titillated or appalled the public and have become part of the city's folklore.

The pages that follow are not for the sick-minded (or by a sick mind, although some have suggested otherwise). And please note, they are not for the fainthearted. They serve as a reminder that the potential for evil, violence and intolerance lurks very close to the surface of even the most benign city environment.

Ugly as it is, Wellington's dark side is a fascinating part of the city. And for those of you who baulk at the prospect of navigating narrow and congested streets by motor vehicle, the good thing is many of the infamous landmarks are close together and can be easily explored on foot. So grab your walking shoes and a stick for poking. The capital's underbelly awaits.

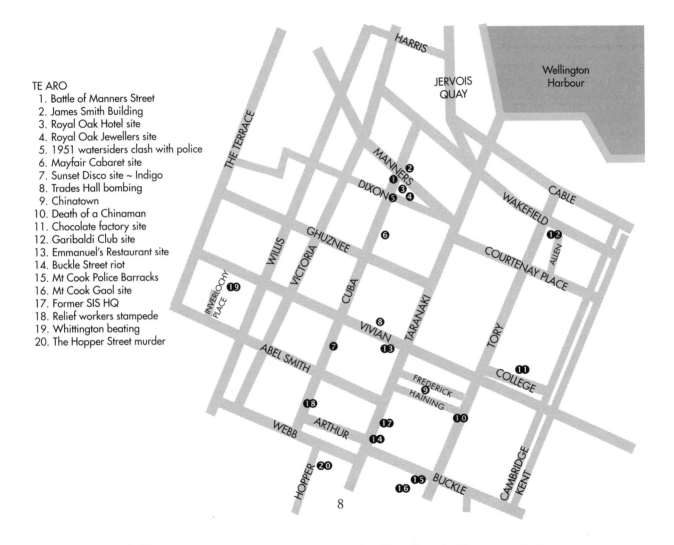

TE ARO
1. Battle of Manners Street
2. James Smith Building
3. Royal Oak Hotel site
4. Royal Oak Jewellers site
5. 1951 watersiders clash with police
6. Mayfair Cabaret site
7. Sunset Disco site ~ Indigo
8. Trades Hall bombing
9. Chinatown
10. Death of a Chinaman
11. Chocolate factory site
12. Garibaldi Club site
13. Emmanuel's Restaurant site
14. Buckle Street riot
15. Mt Cook Police Barracks
16. Mt Cook Gaol site
17. Former SIS HQ
18. Relief workers stampede
19. Whittington beating
20. The Hopper Street murder

Wellington Harbour

HARRIS

JERVOIS QUAY

THE TERRACE

MANNERS

DIXON

WAKEFIELD

CABLE

WILLIS

GHUZNEE

VICTORIA

CUBA

TARANAKI

COURTENAY PLACE

ALLEN

INVERLOCHY PLACE

VIVIAN

ABEL SMITH

TORY

COLLEGE

FREDERICK

HAINING

WEBB

ARTHUR

CAMBRIDGE

KENT

HOPPER

BUCKLE

1.

Te Aro

Modern Te Aro is a lively business and entertainment district ~ a far cry from its notorious past.

The area is one of the very few patches of flat land in Wellington. You'd think that would make it popular among the early settlers. It didn't. Anyone with money or pretensions lived north of Clay Point (the corner of Willis Street and Lambton Quay).

The fact that much of Te Aro's eastern side was a stinky bog didn't do a lot for local property prices during the first years of European settlement. And the early Wellingtonians were quick to complain about the smell and run-down condition of Te Aro Pa, which was in the vicinity of lower Taranaki Street and Manners Street until the 1870s.

An earthquake in 1855 pushed up what would become Courtenay Place, along with the rest of the bog. A population explosion followed, resulting in overcrowding and poor sanitary conditions. Te Aro quickly became a dire slum and a breeding ground for criminals and disease.

Crime, especially theft, was rife ~ the area providing a steady source of inmates for the Mt Cook and Terrace gaols. Opium and illegal gambling in Wellington's Chinatown ~ found in one of the most rundown parts of the slum ~ provided additional attractions for the criminally inclined, as well as a target for racial hatred.

Disease, Te Aro's other scourge, showed its poxy face most visibly in 1918. Wellington was the hardest hit of New Zealand cities by the Spanish Flu epidemic of that year. Many of its flu deaths were recorded in Te Aro's run-down boarding houses. Grotty side streets like Martin Square, off Taranaki Street, had the highest body count.

The area, which among its many notorious attractions is home to Wellington's red light district (*see* chapter 3), maintained its seedy reputation well into the 20th century. It took the emergence of Courtenay Place nightlife in the early 1990s and an inner-city apartment boom to make the area finally fashionable.

Te Aro, Wellington in 1857, looking along Manners Street towards Mount Victoria with the Te Aro foreshore on the left, and the Wesleyan Chapel on the right. Detail inset: Te Aro Pa.
Alexander Turnbull Library F2961 1/2

Some of the last remaining glimpses of early Te Aro can be found in Cuba Street's upper blocks. The area, which features some of Wellington's oldest architecture, hasn't shaken the slum tag. It is very dilapidated and, like the Te Aro of old, a rookery for criminals. The uppermost blocks are waiting for the proposed bypass that will slice through the area from the existing motorway. Transit New Zealand has acquired the heritage buildings in the path of the bypass, allowing them to fall into disrepair, adding to the squalor.

1. Battle of Manners Street ~ Manners & Cuba Streets

An extension of Victoria Street in 1977 cut a swathe through Manners Street. Among the buildings pushed off the map by bulldozers was 43 Manners Street ~ the site of the Allied Services Club in 1943. The club was the ignition point for what became known as the Battle of Manners Street ~ an all-out brawl between US

US troops on manoeuvres in Oriental Bay.
Alexander Turnbull Library F45134 1/2

servicemen and local menfolk that was rumoured to have resulted in several deaths.

The authorities moved quickly to hush up the events (not good for the war effort), which makes it difficult to piece together what actually happened on the evening of 3 April 1943. It seems the brawl started inside the Allied Services Club at around 6pm, then spilled out onto the street ~ spreading to Royal Oak Corner and up Cuba Street as other servicemen and civilians joined in. There were reports of civilians jumping off trams to get involved. The mêlée, however, wasn't just Kiwis against Yanks. Once the fight started, inter-service rivalry between the US Marines and Navy took over ~ the two sides taking the opportunity to settle their differences with their fists.

How the fight inside the Allied Services Club started, is unclear. One version is that drunk Kiwi merchant seamen decided to attack some US marines drinking in the club. Another has it that the fight started between US servicemen and local Maori ~ between whom bad blood had been building for some time.

There was certainly no shortage of Kiwi men wanting to have a go at the Yanks, who, based in camps at Paekakariki and Silverstream, had started arriving on New Zealand shores in 1942. The local men were jealous of the nattily dressed and well-paid Americans, and especially of their allure to Wellington women. There were hundreds of divorce cases resulting from local girls succumbing to their charms (another statistic the government refused to allow the newspapers to print). They were dubbed the 'bedroom commandos'.

Some GIs from the southern states, further fuelling the antagonism, treated local Maori with the same disdain they showed African Americans in their own country during the days of segregation ~ for example, expecting them to walk, rather than take trams.

The brawling moved up Cuba Street as far as the Bristol Hotel (close to the corner of Ghuznee Street) before civilian and military police waded in with truncheons. The authorities had things under control by about 8pm, although skirmishes continued until the final trains departed for the Paekakariki camps at midnight.

Despite the rumours, police reports indicate there were no deaths from the incident. There were four civilian arrests ~ at least one for inciting violence. Locals woke up the next day to find barricades around Manners Street and the area strewn with broken glass.

2. James Smith Building ~ Lower Cuba Street

The James Smith Building was the furthermost building damaged in the Depression riot of 10 May 1931 that started outside the gates of Parliament (*see* Central City No 13 for background).

3. Royal Oak Hotel site ~ Oaks complex, 71-81 Cuba Street

The Royal Oak Hotel, which covered the entire block between Manners Street and Dixon Street, had the reputation as the roughest watering hole in Wellington before its demolition in 1979. There were three main bars ~ the public bar, the bistro and the tavern bar. The hotel was a favourite haunt for lesbians, gay men and transvestites. Micheal Avanti, later convicted of killing a Wellington homosexual (*see* Central City, No 2), robbed gay men he picked up at the hotel. In his autobiography, Avanti wrote of fights at the pub between prostitutes and queens who had

James Smith Building, on the corner of Cuba and Manners Streets.

"make-up on partly unshaven faces and ill-fitting and multicoloured dresses", describing the public bar as "thick with smoke and noise" and providing for a "motley and manifold group of criminals, prostitutes, ship molls and hoboes". Despite the heavy scene, the hotel was trendy among Wellington's 'in-crowd'.

4. Royal Oak Jewellers site ~ Oaks Complex, 71-81 Cuba Street

A botched robbery of Royal Oak Jewellers led to the shooting of 27-year-old Paul Miet on 10 March 1972. It made Dean Wickliffe ~ a violent career criminal with a track record of failed robberies ~ a headline name. His life sentence for the killing is the main reason he has the dubious distinction of spending longer behind bars (more than 30 years) than anyone else in New Zealand.

13

Wickliffe leaving the High Court after his conviction for the murder of Paul Miet.
Alexander Turnbull Library Evening Post collection
1972/2210/7A

fill a duffle bag with rings. Hearing that the shop's proprietor André Miet and his son Paul were upstairs on the mezzanine floor, he ordered them down. When Paul reached the bottom he pushed himself in front of Wickliffe ~ demanding that he leave, and giving his dad the opportunity to rush to the door and shout for help. A shot rang out while Miet senior was at the entrance. Wickliffe made it out to the street, but was tackled by two passers-by who had heard the father's calls for help. The gun went off again during the scuffle ~ the bullet hitting a window across the street. Wickliffe was disarmed and pinned to the ground. Paul Miet died in an ambulance on the way to hospital.

Wickliffe claimed Miet had lunged at him, causing the Luger to go off by accident. The jury didn't buy it. He was convicted of murder and given life. Wickliffe later got hold of police notes, under the Official Information Act, that reported the shop assistant saying Miet had indeed lunged at him. When Wickliffe had his request for an appeal turned down, he went on a hunger

The jewellers' shop (formerly 79 Cuba Street) is no longer there ~ demolished to make way for the present retail complex. The shop may be gone, but there are few Wellingtonians from the time who don't vividly remember the day's events.

Wickliffe walked into the jewellers about 8.45am carrying a Luger pistol, his face masked by a grey woollen balaclava. He ordered the shop assistant to strike. After intervention by the government he got his appeal, which reduced his conviction to manslaughter, but didn't lift the original life sentence ~ leaving him very bitter.

He was finally released on parole in 1987, although his freedom didn't last long. A few months later he was convicted of involvement in an armed hold-up of a video store in Onehunga, earning himself another seven and a half years in Paremoremo.

Out on parole again in 1996, Wickliffe was arrested for the murder of a Mount Maunganui man, the prosecution alleging he had shot him for being a police nark following a raid on the man's house for cannabis. Wickliffe was found guilty (becoming the first person in New Zealand to be twice convicted of murder), but got off on a technicality when the Court of Appeal overturned the verdict because TV3 had screened a television programme about him during the trial.

Wickliffe's other claim to fame is as the only prisoner to have escaped from Paremoremo twice. He became the first person to escape the maximum security prison after using a home-made rope to scale the fences in 1976. He was recaptured in a nearby marsh only a couple of kilometres from the prison.

In 1991, taking a prison boilermaker hostage, Wickliffe was more successful in his second breakout ~ spending nearly five weeks on the run before recapture. He claimed his two escapes were intended to highlight an unjust sentence.

5.   1951 watersiders clash with police ~ corner Cuba & Dixon Streets

A line of police stopped some 1000 marching watersiders at the intersection on 2 May 1951. They had left Trades Hall intent on marching to Parliament to meet with the government, which was refusing to speak with them. It took about 100 police to stop the march. Batons started swinging before Jock Barnes, firebrand president of the recently deregistered Waterside Workers Union, raised on the shoulders of his fellow strikers, called for the group to stop.

The strikers carried a banner saying "A Police State is the New Order" ~ a pretty accurate summary of the political climate during the waterfront strike, which lasted 151 days in 1951.

The strike started when employers refused to allow the watersiders a 15% wage increase, granted by the Arbitration Court. The union responded by imposing a ban on overtime. The National government of the day then stepped in, declaring a state of emergency, deregistering the Watersiders' Union and allowing servicemen to unload the ships. The strikers jeered as the ring-in wharfies struggled with the loads.

The emergency regulations gave the police unprecedented power to clamp down on the strikers. They could arrest picketers. The strikers were forbidden to hold public meetings and marches. One of the new regulations even made it an offence to give food to strikers or their families.

The government also placed restrictions on the media, preventing publication of watersiders' views. The biased coverage painted the strikers as communist sympathisers wishing to undermine the Korean war effort. Prime minister Sid Holland ranted about the "enemy within." Watersiders tried in vain to present their side of the story to the public, including using homemade radios to broadcast their message and printing posters and leaflets. Detectives began

151 days

FACSIMILE EDITION

Official history of the great waterfront lockout and supporting strikes, February 15—July 15, 1951

by DICK SCOTT

foreword by JOCK BARNES

raiding homes at night to confiscate the printing presses.

The government's campaign did the trick. Watersiders found themselves marginalised, particularly when Labour Party MPs sided with the government, and the Federation of Labour, which had split with the militant union earlier that year, refused its support. The strike finally came to an end on 12 July. The National Party used the opportunity to call a snap election. It returned to power with an increased majority, taking the result as a mandate to impose its conservative agenda on the lives of New Zealanders ~ including the re-introduction of hanging and the start of oppressive censorship of music, movies and literature.

6.   Mayfair Cabaret site ~ 91 Cuba Street

The Mayfair Cabaret used to occupy the light green concrete building just up from the Dixon Street intersection. On 12 May 1945, just four days after VE Day, the club was the scene of a second big scrap between US and New Zealand servicemen (*see* No 1 for background on the first).

The fight started when a group of Maori soldiers claimed some American sailors had stolen their hats. A large crowd of Maori troops, on leave from the army camp at Trentham, caught wind of the row and tried to join in. The sailors held them back by throwing broken furniture from the upstairs windows. A US medical officer arrived at the scene, only to have his jeep upturned by an angry Maori. After brawling (joined by civilians) with an American shore patrol, they eventually moved off, allowing the sailors to scurry back to their ship.

7. Sunset Disco site ~ Indigo, 171 Cuba Street

The deep blue entrance to the Indigo bar and nightclub stands about halfway between Dixon and Vivian Streets. The site has a long and colourful history as a Wellington nightspot. It has been Ali Baba's, the Cave, the Tokyo Bar, among other names. In the early 1980s it was the Sunset Disco. It was there that 30-year-old amputee John Morgan fatally stabbed Sinclair Inglis, 24, after an argument in the early hours of Christmas

Site of the Sunset Disco in Cuba Street, where John Morgan stabbed Sinclair Inglis.

Eve 1982. The killing led to a mad, action movie-like car chase through Lower Hutt and Wainuiomata, and a police shooting that attracted its own fire in the form of public criticism about trigger-happy cops.

Morgan's Land Rover was spotted the day after the stabbing at the Silverstream tip. He rammed a police car to escape, squeezing past a large compactor rubbish truck blocking the road. Then, chased by a police helicopter with a dog handler, he crashed through ten roadblocks before veering off the Coast Road outside Wainuiomata into farm property. He forded the Wainuiomata River, finally stopping the Land Rover on a stony bank at the other side of the stream. Seeing that the patrol cars couldn't follow, Morgan got out and waved a large axe at his pursuers.

The police helicopter was able to land close by. A dog handler jumped out and drew his gun, demanding that the fugitive surrender. Morgan turned and threw the axe, hitting the constable in the face, knocking him unconscious. The blow caused the cop to fire an involuntary shot ~ hitting Morgan's artificial foot. Another officer across the bank fired, hitting Morgan in the chest, killing him almost instantly.

The police were heavily criticised for the shooting ~

John Morgan leading his 'action movie' chase on the Silverstream tip road. The ride ended with the police shooting Morgan.
Alexander Turnbull Library Dominion Post collection 1982/5031/7

particularly for dropping a young constable into the thick of it and for shooting a one-legged man who didn't have a firearm and wasn't likely to run very far. Their actions, however, were later vindicated by an internal police inquiry and the Solicitor General.

8. Trades Hall bombing ~ 126 Vivian Street

A grey concrete arch frames the entrance to Trades Hall ~ home to some of the country's most staunchly left-wing unions. In 1984 it was the scene of one of the very few political bombings in New Zealand's history, and one for which there has never been an arrest, despite a massive investigation.

On 27 March, around 5.15pm, an explosion blasted the front doors off their hinges and showered the pavement with broken glass. Among the débris blown onto the street was a dachshund called Patch ~ burnt and blinded by the blast, but alive. Patch's owner Ernie Abbott, the building's 63-year-old caretaker, wasn't so lucky. A bystander who ran into the smoke-filled building found his badly burned and mangled body among the wreckage, looking "as if a pile of paper had been set on fire and a dummy had been thrown on top."

Fragments of material revealed the hiding place for

Trades Hall in Vivian Street.

19

the bomb – a worn and faded light-green suitcase with a rare Rica banana sticker on its side. Union officials had spotted the case on the morning of the blast, but fortunately for them hadn't moved it. Abbott triggered a booby-trap – a mercury switch – when he tried to shift or open the case, detonating what was thought to be three sticks of gelignite.

Police identified the prime suspect as a European man in his mid to late 40s, seen on the corner of Taranaki Street and Vivian Street carrying a small suitcase on the morning of the bombing. They interviewed several people, but no one checked out as the culprit. A new lead emerged in late 2001 when an informant alerted Wellington police that the daughter of a suspect lied to police during the original investigation. The informant claimed that the daughter, after falling out with her dad and wrestling with her conscience, was now saying the

In the 1970s Ernie Abbott led a deputation to government on behalf of the Cleaners & Caretakers' Union to complain about rising prices: cauliflowers had gone from 59 cents to $1.40 in two weeks.
Alexander Turnbull Library Dominion Post collection 1977/3688/4

famous suitcase belonged to her. As yet, there have been no arrests.

There were many theories about the motive for the bombing. There had been a wildcat strike by bus drivers the day before, and the bomb had been placed near the Tramways Union office in the building. The Federation of Labour could have been the target – it had been reported (wrongly) that the group's hierarchy was due to meet in the building. There was even talk that the culprit was a right-wing Asian government that had a rabid hatred for unions and wanted to make sure prime minister Rob Muldoon stayed in power. Taking the other extreme, there were murmurs that the union movement had planted the bomb itself in order to gain sympathy at a time when anti-union sentiment was high. And it was suggested the blast was intended to stop the printing of leaflets supporting anti-nuclear protester Dr Helen Caldicott (there was a print room in Trades Hall very close to the blast).

David Lange, then leader of the Labour Party, and many notable union leaders were among the 2500 mourners at Abbott's funeral, held at the Wellington Town Hall on 3 April. Union members around the country stopped work as a mark of respect.

Ernie Abbott's plaque in Cobblestone Park, Vivian Street.

There is a tree planted in Abbott's honour, marked by a plaque, in Cobblestone Park across the road from Trades Hall. Inside the foyer of the hall there is a commemorative seat, crafted from timber collected from the ruins of the blast.

9. Chinatown ~ Frederick & Haining Streets

The two streets featured rows of dilapidated, single-storey huts in the late 19th century ~ home to Wellington's Chinese population and the target of scorn by Europeans.

THE YELLOW PERIL.

The era was one of extreme xenophobia and discrimination. The hard-working Chinese were seen to be taking jobs from the working class. There were fears of the 'yellow peril' invading the South Pacific. Children were warned to steer clear of the area for fear of catching all manner of diseases, or being boiled alive to make preserved ginger. And there was righteous indignation about opium smoking and illegal gambling dens.

There was some truth behind the opium and gambling stories. Both Chinese and Europeans used the area for the illicit activities ~ the opium dens surviving right up to the 1950s. The Opium Act made the drug illegal in 1901, leading to police raids. Smokers tried to thwart the raids by introducing secret knocks, along with hidden entrances in stairwells with steel doors that the police couldn't break down ~ giving enough time to hide the pipes, scales and other drug paraphernalia. Police would sometimes bypass the doors to get into the dens by smashing a hole in the roof or bashing down an adjoining door.

One of the most popular gambling games was the pakapoo lottery ~ an early form of Lotto. The gambler would buy a ticket with eighty numbers and mark ten of them. The winners were those whose marked numbers matched a sealed master card. Another game was fantan ~ played by betting on whether the number of copper coins covered by a cup was odd or even.

Very little remains of the original Chinatown. There are a few landmarks down Frederick Street, including the former Chinese Mission Hall (46 Frederick Street), built by the Anglican church, the former Chinese Masonic Hall (23 Frederick Street), and the Tung Jung Association Building (2 Frederick Street), constructed as a community hall in 1926.

The Anglican Chinese Mission Hall in Frederick Street, a vestige of Wellington's Chinatown and the activities of the Church Mission a century ago.
Susan Maclean *Architect of the Angels* Steele Roberts 2003

"It wasn't there on Friday night when we left," said one of the workmen engaged on demolition of 48 Haining Street. Surrounded by pakapoo tickets, this hole in the floorboards mysteriously appeared during the weekend. It was suspected that Chinese were still visiting the premises looking for gambling caches.
Alexander Turnbull Library F43234 1/2

10. Death of a 'Chinaman' ~ corner Haining & Tory Streets

Hatred of Wellington's Chinese population reached its extreme in September 1905. Witnesses saw a man with a revolver walk up to Joe Kum Yung ~ an elderly and penniless former goldminer from the West Coast who was strolling along eating a bag of peanuts ~ and fire two shots at point blank range at his head outside 13 Haining Street, close to the corner of Tory Street.

Kum Yung died later at hospital. He had been shot the day before he was due to board a ship to return

RIVALRY IN THE FRUIT TRADE.

The Orange Boy: 'Ere y'are! 'ere y'are! Eight for a shilling. If yer buys 'em off the bloomin' Chow yer gets 13 and a dose er leprosy thrown in.

A curiously conflicting blend of virtue and weakness, Lionel Terry has gone to his grave in Dunedin as New Zealand's criminal curiosity of this century. This reconstruction of his story, made with the help of his friends, doctor and newspaper reports, does not seek to judge him, for that was done nearly half a century ago. It merely shows some of the pieces of the fantastic jigsaw of his character, but does not assemble them. Not even Terry could do that.

Here is the beginning of the Terry story, No. 13 Haining Street, Wellington, photographed last week. It was outside this house at No. 13 that Lionel Terry shot an aged Chinese in 1905 to focus attention on the "yellow peril." The cross indicates the entrance to No. 13. Terry was a mounted policeman in Africa at the time of the historic Jameson raid, later saw service in the Matabele War, and was personally known to Cecil Rhodes and Kruger. Between these trips he studied art in London.

The Strange Story Of Lionel Terry

Alexander Turnbull Library

home. After the shooting the gunman ran off towards Taranaki Street, but gave himself up to police the next morning. He was Lionel Terry, an upper-crust English surveyor, educated at Eton and Oxford, and employed by the Department of Lands and Survey.

The shooting turned out to be a brutal publicity stunt for Terry's anti-immigration views, which he had published in a pamphlet called *The Shadow*. He claimed to have no grudge against Kum Yung and had only picked on him because he was crippled and old -

"whose existence was a painful burden". He was sentenced to death; but, as a result of several public petitions for mercy, that was commuted to life imprisonment. After trying to burn down the Lyttelton Gaol, he spent the remainder of his life at the Sunnyside and Seacliff mental hospitals, dying in 1952 aged 79.

Terry was insane, but the scary thing was many New Zealanders shared his extreme views well into the 20th century. During his stay at Sunnyside a petition demanding his release attracted 5000 signatures.

Lionel Terry

11. Adams Bruce chocolate factory site ~ 16 College Street

The Adams Bruce chocolate factory used to be based in the Fletcher Trust building (14-18 College Street). Miles Radcliffe, the factory's mild-mannered 50-year-old manager, was found bashed and strangled on 6 February 1946 in a side doorway of the building. Radcliffe was a homosexual who regularly took men back to his office in the evenings for sex. The pathologist found he had been sexually aroused just before the beating. Police suspected foreign seamen, after witness accounts of two men near the factory and the finding of foreign matches near the body. The murder was never solved.

12. Garibaldi Club site ~ Pan-Hellenic Association Building, corner Wakefield & Allen Streets

Angelo La Mattina, a 23-year-old Italian plumber, bashed the part-time caretaker of the club to death with a bottle at the Garibaldi Club in 1957 for making a move on his girlfriend. La Mattina ended up with a death sentence for murder, but was spared the noose

by a general election. National had re-introduced hanging in 1950; Labour vowed to scrap it. Luckily for La Mattina, Labour won the 1957 election ~ by a mere two seats. He was deported to Italy in 1968 and later wrote to former Labour prime minister Walter Nash to say thanks for saving his life.

The Garibaldi Club was based at the time in the top storey of the cream-coloured Pan-Hellenic Association Building. The latest incarnation of the club, a meeting place for Wellington's Italian community, can be found on the corner of Vivian Street and Tory Street.

13. Greek tragedy ~ Emmanuel's Restaurant site, 41 Vivian Street

Restaurant owner Emmanuel 'Manny' Papadopoulos, 37, died in controversial circumstances on 30 December 1989 ~ suffocating on a city street while being restrained by police.

Papadopoulos, according to his sister, left the restaurant to check out patronage at the Arena nightclub in Wakefield Street (259 Wakefield Street,

26

now the site of Silverscreen Films). He wanted to see whether it was worth keeping the restaurant open. Police stopped him near the Arena around 2.50am when they noticed his taillights weren't working. The minor traffic infringement became something a lot bigger when the Greek restaurateur put a plastic bag containing about 10 grams of cocaine in his mouth, pushed the officer aside and bolted down the street.

The Arena's manager and assistant manager saw Papadopoulos sprint by, chased by a police sergeant and two traffic officers. They watched as he was slammed against a steel building site wall and wrestled to the ground, and said that the sergeant was holding him around the throat while restraining him (the police denied it was a choker hold). Papadopoulos died on the footpath, two weeks before the birth of his third child.

The outraged Papadopoulos family disputed autopsy results that Emmanuel had choked on the bag of cocaine, blaming excessive use of force by the police, backed by findings that the restraining hold had damaged the hyoid bone in his neck.

The public outcry saw the newly formed Police Complaints Authority undertake this as its first hearing.

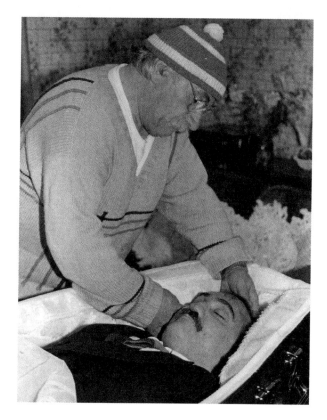

Emmanuel Papadopoulos Snr adjusting the head of his dead son.
Alexander Turnbull Library Evening Post collection 1990/0009/10A

It, along with the Wellington Coroner, decided that death was due to asphyxia, the result of swallowing the bag. That conclusion backed the findings of two pathologists. But, muddying the waters, two other pathologists contradicted that finding ~ one saying the more probable cause of death was force applied to Papadopoulos's neck, the other believing the restraining hold may have prevented him from coughing up the bag.

The authority's report rejected witness accounts that the police sergeant continued holding Papadopoulos around his throat after he stopped struggling. And it questioned the credibility of witnesses in the crowd that gathered while the scuffle was taking place, saying some of them were Greek and knew Papadopoulos.

Emmanuel's closed in 1991. The building is currently occupied by a Thai restaurant. Not long after the case a graffiti was seen on a city wall: "You can't have your coke and eat it too."

14. Buckle Street riot ~
corner Buckle & Taranaki Streets

The corner was the scene of a violent riot on 3 November 1913 involving police and supporters of the striking watersiders (*see* Central City, No 9 for background). A large crowd had gathered to jeer military and police staff guarding the special constables at the old Mt Cook prison site (*see* No 16). Things tuned nasty when the crowd started throwing bricks, iron bolts, old horseshoes and other missiles at the police. The police tried to disperse the crowd with a fire hose, which worked for a while, but the mob came back and resumed the fusillade. A charge by horsemen down Buckle Street finally cleared the crowd.

There were reports of shots from Arthur Street and an upstairs window in Taranaki Street. One of the rioters was later accused of trying to murder the police commissioner. Witnesses reported he had fired some shots just before the hosing started, but he was later acquitted. Two soldiers suffered bullet wounds during the riots; neither was seriously injured.

15. Mt Cook Police Barracks ~
corner Tory & Buckle Streets

This brick building was opened in 1893 to ensure a police presence close to Wellington's slum areas. It was on the doorstep of the city's despised Chinatown and not too far down the road from Newtown ~ at that

The new pavilion at Basin Reserve c.1928,
with Mt Cook Gaol building in the background.
Alexander Turnbull Library F82622 1/2

time one of the most crowded suburbs in the country and the stomping ground for gangs of young larrikins. The most well-known of the gangs was the Feather Push, which marked the scene of its crimes with a roughly drawn feather.

The station was built by convict labour with bricks fired next door at the Mt Cook Gaol. Many of the bricks visible from the street bear the government 'arrow' symbol. That's unusual, as such bricks would normally face inwards, hiding the arrows from view. The building closed as a police station in 1956.

16. Mt Cook Gaol site ~ Buckle Street (next to old police station)

The former National War Memorial Museum stands on the site of the Mt Cook Gaol (along with what's left of the hill that was once Mt Cook itself). Construction finished in 1882, creating what the locals regarded as an eyesore.

Like the adjacent police station, convict labour did the building work, using bricks made on the site. Some of the more enterprising labourers took the opportunity to make counterfeit coins, using a press that had been smuggled onto the site. They rolled the fake florins into

Mt Cook Police Barracks, from which police kept a watchful eye on the Te Aro slum.

balls of clay, dropping them on the ground during their march back to the Terrace Gaol (*see* Other infamous city sites, No 2) to be picked up by former convicts. The police eventually busted the operation, which turned out to have been masterminded by a couple of Americans.

The prison closed in 1903. The building then found

30

use as an army barracks – housing the special police recruits during the violent watersiders' strike of 1913 (see Central City, No 9 and Te Aro, No 14). Much to the relief of its detractors, the building was finally demolished in 1930 to make way for the new museum.

There was also a public execution on the site some 30 years before the construction of the famous gaol – one of only eight in New Zealand history before the gory spectacle was outlawed in 1858.

William Good was hanged on 17 June 1850 for killing a seaman and hiding his body in a brine barrel aboard a ship in the Wellington port. The scaffold was erected outside the brick walls of an earlier gaol, attracting a large crowd. They watched a "black man who had arrived in the colony about two years ago"

Tasman Street treat:
bricks fired at the
Mt Cook Gaol.
Ben Steele

carry out the execution, according to newspaper reports. He revealed his lack of experience by pushing the lever that released the trapdoor the wrong way. The crowd was stunned when nothing happened. A warder had to intervene to carry out the death sentence.

17. Former Security Intelligence Service HQ – 175 Taranaki Street (corner of Martin Square)

Protestors pelted the former Security Intelligence Service HQ building, now the home of an engine reconditioning workshop, with paint bombs, fruit and chunks of wood during a march on 14 October 1977. The massive crowd, which numbered as many as 20,000, had marched from Parliament to oppose a law change giving the SIS more power to snoop on citizens. The protestors didn't get past the line of police outside the building, but managed to smash some windows with their missiles. At the time, just retired SIS head Brigadier Gilbert was loathed second only to Rob Muldoon among those challenging the authoritarian politics of the day. There were six arrests.

The SIS HQ has since shifted to levels 7 & 8 of Defence House in Stout Street.

The SIS headquarters in Taranaki St
were a target of frequent protests ~
note the paintbomb splatters.
Dominion Post collection

18. Relief workers stampede ~ Upper Cuba Street

A vacant section on Upper Cuba Street near the corner of Arthur Street (exact site unknown) was the scene of the second and final big stoush between police and striking Wellington relief workers in 1932.

Some 2000 strikers gathered on the section to hear their delegates speak, despite a ban on public meetings, on 11 May ~ the day after a mob of unemployed workers had rampaged down Lambton Quay and Willis Street (See Central City, No 13 for background).

It's unclear exactly what happened, but reports suggest the police tried to stop one of the speakers, inciting jeers from the crowd. When stones started to rain down, 50 foot police and six mounted officers charged with their batons, causing a stampede that saw the men jumping fences and fleeing through the backyards of adjacent houses. The only serious reported injury was a broken leg ~ suffered when a fence collapsed during the stampede. An inquiry by the Minister of Justice later exonerated the police from accusations they had used excessive force, despite nearly 100 affidavits saying otherwise.

19. Whittington beating ~ Inverlochy Place

The murder of a purple-haired 14-year-old in Inverlochy Place exposed the grimy underbelly of the upper Te Aro area in May 1999.

Jason Meads and Stephen Smith, both in their mid-20s, gave Wellington High School student Jeff

Whittington a fatal kicking in the small lane off Abel Smith Street in the early hours of 8 May. They had picked up Whittington, sleepy and stumbling from the effects of the hallucinogenic plant datura, in a car in Vivian Street ~ allegedly because they didn't like his homosexual looks. Whittington's battered body was found lying in a puddle in the carpark outside the Inverlochy Art School, where Meads and Smith had dragged him from the car. He died in Wellington Hospital the next day. The two bragged about the assault later that morning to parlour workers at the Kensington Inn (*see* Red Light District, No 8). Both were convicted of murder.

20. The Hopper Street murder

Rufus Marsh and Dennis Luke are two of New Zealand's most violent criminals. Their brutal handiwork first attracted headlines when a New Zealand Distributors employee found the badly beaten body of a pensioner under a pallet outside the roller doors of a loading bay on Hopper Street on 12 November 1974.

Police tracked down the teenage killers ~ Marsh, 19, and Dennis Luke, 16 ~ by following bloody footprints to a house up the street. Marsh passed most of the blame to his young mate, saying 59-year-old Joseph 'Taffy' Williamson had provoked the beating with a tirade of insults when they passed him on the street. Despite the severity of Williamson's head injuries and the fact the teenagers had done nothing to save his life as he lay injured, Marsh got away with a manslaughter conviction. Luke got life for murder.

Both men went on to kill again. Marsh was found guilty of the ghastly killing of a Mt Victoria woman in 1986 (*see* Other infamous city sites, No 7). And Luke, who went on to become president of the Hawera chapter of Black Power, earned himself another murder rap for his role in the gang-related shooting of prosecution witness Chris Crean in 1996.

A plumbing and bathroom supplier now occupies the site (57-61 Hopper Street) where Williamson's life ebbed away. You can find the location about halfway up the eastern side of Hopper Street, across the road from the Arlington Apartments.

2.
Red light district

Wellington's red light district is never going to rival Bangkok's Patpong Road or Amsterdam's *Walletjes* ~ at least, not for size. But it is unique… Jody Hanson, a Waikato University academic, suggested in 1996 that Vivian and Cuba Streets should be marketed as an international tourism attraction ~ as the "world's smallest red light district". Carmen, the former Wellington transsexual entertainer, has expressed similar thoughts.

The sex industry is big business for Wellington that seems to be growing. Hanson estimated it to be worth $5.2 million a year to the capital in 1996. More recent estimates put the figure at around $30 million, taking into account the hundreds of prostitutes working outside the registered parlours. It's going to be interesting to see what effect the 2003 law change decriminalising prostitution will have on the industry ~ especially in the face of dire warnings from existing brothel owners fearing an explosion of unscrupulous operators.

1.   Where the red light glows ~ Vivian Street

The blocks between Cuba Street and Taranaki Street form Wellington's red light district ~ although that title may be challenged in future years as strip bars and brothels move into another parts of the city, most recently Courtenay Place (see No 9). As it stands, Vivian Street doesn't have a lot to justify its sleazy reputation ~ former mayor Mark Blumsky dismissed it as "16 light bulbs, two street corners and five girls" in 1996. Most of the city's parlours and escort agencies are not based on Vivian Street, although many are nearby. There's only one strip bar ~ Liks (*see* No 3), and streetwalkers are more likely to be found around the corner in Marion Street.

Vivian Street's red light history dates back to the 19th century when it was called Ingestre Street and featured a cluster of brothels. By the 1970s it had become one of the most notorious streets in Wellington. That decade was the heyday of grotty, but big name, strip clubs like the Purple Onion (see

RED LIGHT DISTRICT
1. Where the red light glows ~ Vivian Street
2. Club Exotique site
3. Liks
4. Purple Onion site
5. Evergreen Coffee House
6. Streetwalker haunt
7. Carmen's International Coffee Lounge
8. Kensington Inn
9. Mermaid Bar and Splash Club
10. Sanctuary

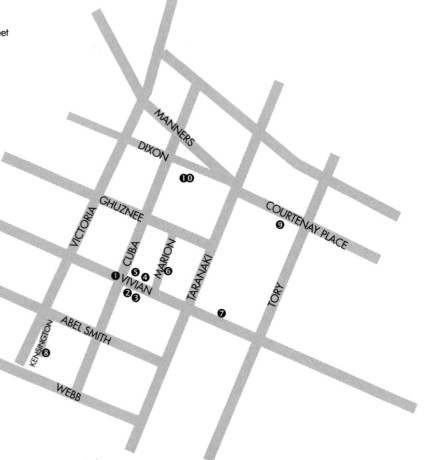

No 4). The sex industry was then dominated by gangs and drugs. Vivian Street is a lot cleaner these days, which many attribute to Brian Le Gros ~ who, before selling up in 2004, had owned red light businesses in the area for some 30 years, notably the Hole in the Wall, the Purple Onion and Liks. Le Gros espoused a 'no drugs, no weapons' policy.

This sign in Vivian Street is all that remains of one of Wellington's first strip clubs.

2.   Club Exotique site ~ 149 Vivian Street

An old shop sign above the entrance to the Ceroc Dance Studio is all that remains of one of Wellington's first strip clubs ~ Club Exotique. It opened in early 1960s at 98 Manners Street, near the corner of Cuba Mall, and moved a few years later to the Vivian Street site, finally closing in the late 1980s.

3.   Liks ~ 143-147 Vivian Street

The former Salvation Army building is the most visible of Vivian Street's red-light edifices. It's fittingly bright red and, until changing hands in September 2004, had been owned by strip club king Brian Le Gros, who's had more influence than anyone on adult entertainment in Wellington.

Le Gros turned the broken-down Salvation Army building into Tiffanys and started an adult cabaret show in 1982. Tiffanys even made a foray into international sport sponsorship when it helped fund Wellington swimmer Toni Jeffs's Olympic campaign in 1992, attracting controversy for Jeffs. When punters started saying Tiffanys had become boring Le Gros created the Liks strip bar in the mid-'90s. He started the Ladies Bar downstairs, featuring male strippers, for female

customers. He closed it three years later, saying he found the female clientele difficult to handle, and opened the Cigar Bar ~ a bar and brothel ~ in its place. Faced with urgent building repairs, Le Gros shut down the Cigar Bar in May 2004.

Le Gros and Liks have had their brushes with the law over the years. Liks came close to losing its liquor licence in 1998 after employing an underage stripper. More recently, Le Gros's claims to spurn drugs and violence suffered a credibility blow during the trial for the drug-related killing of Terri King ~ who used to work at Liks while going out with one of the strippers.

King was shot in the head, execution style, on 13 April 1999 in the Tararua Ranges. William Haanstra ~ a 23 year old model ~ was charged with his killing, but acquitted after a High Court trial. Investigating police searched Liks, seizing a rifle and ammunition. They also seized other firearms in locked garages belonging to Le Gros.

During Haanstra's trial, a witness said that Le Gros

asked for King to be "fucked up" while buying ecstasy tablets in South Africa. Defence lawyers went so far to suggest Le Gros could have put a contract out on King. Denied a chance to appear on the witness stand, Le Gros told the *Evening Post* he asked a South African former police officer to scare King and take his drugs, but not arrest him, saying he didn't want King to get into trouble and that he hated the drug trade. The murder remains unsolved.

Angry at the Wellington City Council's refusal to allow him to set up shop in Courtenay Place (see No 9), Le Gros has since shifted to Auckland.

4.   Purple Onion site ~ 140 Vivian Street

The Purple Onion was Wellington's most notorious strip-club in the 1970s. The first red light venue in the city to feature a 'Les Girls' transvestite act, former employees remember it as sleazy and violent. Many of the strippers moonlighted as hookers, loitering after their acts to pick up customers. And because of strict licensing laws, the club was one of the few places where alcohol was served after 10pm ~ from under the counter.

Among the strippers was well-known transsexual Carmen ~ then Trevor Rupe ~ who also worked the footpath outside the club before starting her International Coffee Lounge (*see* No 7), taking her clients into the unlit side alleys for what she called "short-time knee tremblers". Georgina Beyer, another famous Wellington transsexual, now an MP, also stripped at the Purple Onion while still a man. She writes in her autobiography about using adhesive tape to hide her wedding tackle during dance routines.

Former Liks owner Brian Le Gros bought the club when it was in its death throes in late 1970s, initially starting a dragshow, then turning it into a private club. When those ventures failed, he closed it down, later establishing the Playgirls massage and sauna parlour on the site. A café that opened in 2000 around the corner in Cuba Street has adopted the Purple Onion name in homage to the glory days of the former strip club.

5.   Evergreen Coffee House ~ 146 Vivian Street

The late-night coffee bar provided shelter from Wellington's dodgy weather for prostitutes working in the Vivian Street area until the recent death of its proprietor. A peephole enabled scrutiny and barring of would-be patrons. Once inside, customers could mingle with well-known sex workers, many of whom had their images adorning the walls, and enjoy an illicit shot of whisky in their coffee.

6. Streetwalker haunt ~ Marion Street

Marion Street, just off Vivian Street, is popular among Wellington's streetwalkers. They're out most nights of the weeks ~ the queens usually bunched down one end, the girls down the other (so customers can tell the difference).

The attraction of Marion Street is pretty obvious. The street is darker and a little bit more discreet for customers than Vivian Street ~ the traditional groin of Wellington's red light district. There's plenty of room for cars to pull up. And the nooks and alleys, particularly along the eastern side, give privacy for business transactions with foot customers, evidenced by the scattering of used condoms some mornings.

Many of the alleys are now blocked at night to stop the trade.

The mural outside Caz Interiors at the corner with Ghuznee Street captures the street's long association with hookers. The artists recruited a real streetwalker to model for the original image of the prostitute leaning against the wall (it's since been updated). The story goes that, keen to take advantage of the marketing opportunity, she took to wearing identical clothes and even changing her hair to match the mural, which had been painted in a different style.

7. Carmen's International Coffee Lounge ~ 86 Vivian Street

It's hard to believe the boring brown box that houses the New Zealand CCS offices is on the site of Carmen's International Coffee Lounge ~ the colourful after-hours nightspot and infamous brothel of the 1970s.

Born Trevor Rupe in Taumarunui, Carmen ran the coffee lounge from 1967 until the late '70s.

She supported herself by prostitution to fund the garish lounge with its plush velvet upholstery, oriental rugs, tropical fish, squawking parrot, and Raphael, Van Dyke and Goldie reproductions on the wall. Situated next to the Salvation Army citadel, Carmen nicknamed the area 'Heaven and Hell'. She claimed politicians among her guests, along with many visiting celebrities.

There were bedrooms upstairs for those who wanted private entertainment with Carmen's hostesses. A ritual known as 'The Cups' allowed customers to indicate their sexual preference without the need for embarrassing conversation. A client wishing to have straight sex would turn their cup upside-down on the saucer. To be entertained by a transvestite or transsexual drag queen, they would place their cup on its side. If they wanted a boy, they would place the saucer on top of the cup. Customers would leave by the front door, meet in the lane besides the building, then re-enter through a discreet door off the lane that led to a concealed staircase.

The police tried on several occasions to catch Carmen and her staff in sex acts with paying customers. She ended up getting a few fines, but the clumsy attempts at entrapment largely ended up with embarrassment for the police and headlines that further fuelled Carmen's notoriety, attracting more customers. Before its demolition in 1978 the lounge had become so well-known that tourists were stopping by to take photos.

Carmen went on to run for the Wellington mayoralty in 1977 ~ her campaign masterminded as a stir by property tycoon Robert Jones. She polled a credible fourth ~ performing better than former mayor Frank Kitts ~ on a platform of guaranteeing gaiety and sunshine. She left for Australia in 1980 ~ by then her flamboyant personality and reputation as the queen of risqué entertainment had been firmly enshrined in Wellington folklore.

8.   Kensington Inn ~ 21 Kensington Street

This unassuming weatherboard house is Wellington's biggest brothel ~ the Kensington Inn. Like many of the city's dens of ill-repute, there is little to distinguish it from its residential neighbours.

Operating since the early 1990s, the Inn is one of 17 brothels (to July 2004) registered in the capital under the new Prostitution Reform Act. It has more than 100 staff on its books. The building, along with another

41

Wellington's biggest brothel, the Kensington Inn.

Te Moananui to put the Euphoria out of business. The Molotov cocktails, thrown by two of Te Moananui's gang associates, set fire to the lounge, but didn't destroy the building, which is no longer a brothel.

Te Moananui's imprisonment for arson ended a reign of gang violence in the city that hadn't been seen in the Wellington area since the 1970s. The former right-hand man of Black Power founder Rei Harris and sergeant-at-arms for the gang had established a breakaway faction that had reignited old animosities with the Mongrel Mob. The warfare culminated in a drive-by shooting of a police van carrying a mob member outside the District Court in Ballance Street in 1996.

9. Mermaid Bar & Splash Club ~ 75 Courtenay Place

The strip bar (Mermaid) and massage parlour upstairs (Splash) are the sole red light businesses in Courtenay Place. They're not going to be joined by any others in the foreseeable future ~ courtesy of a council bylaw in 2001 banning commercial sex premises in the popular entertainment area.

The council fast-tracked the bylaw after a barrage

brothel around the corner, has heritage status and will be relocated if the proposed inner-city bypass goes ahead (which is looking very likely).

The Inn attracted headlines in 1997 when a former manager was prosecuted for ordering the firebombing of a rival brothel ~ the Euphoria, based at 13 Garfield Street, Brooklyn. An ex-Inn employee had set up the Brooklyn operation and was luring staff away from her old employer. Carolyn Bowles was found guilty of hiring maverick Black Power Movement leader Wayne

of protest from local businesses and mayor Mark Blumsky about the opening of Mermaid. Blumsky swore he was going to do whatever he could to stop the area turning into "some kind of Kings Cross". The bylaw was too late to prevent the opening of Splash, which shares 75 Courtenay Place with Mermaid. And the council voted against making the bylaw retrospective ~ effectively giving Mermaid and Splash a monopoly on the area's sex trade. Liks owner Brian Le Gros, who had been refused permission to move to Courtenay Place a few months earlier, was furious about the bylaw. He accused the council of being unpatriotic in giving dibs on the area to the Auckland-based owners of Mermaid and Splash ~ a move he feared could put Liks out of business.

10. Sanctuary ~ 39 Dixon Street

The Sanctuary is a club for gay and bisexual men to meet and have sex on-site. Known by its present name since 1992, it was the first venue of its kind in Wellington. The club attracted headlines in July 1994 when a Heretaunga College teacher was found dead on the premises. The post-mortem revealed cardiac arrest; the pathologist saying it wasn't triggered by a heart stimulant sold at the club.

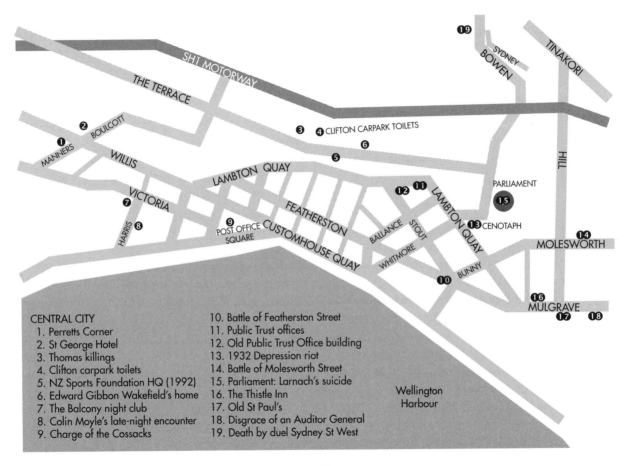

SH1 MOTORWAY

THE TERRACE

SYDNEY
BOWEN
TINAKORI

CLIFTON CARPARK TOILETS

BOULCOTT

MANNERS

WILLIS

LAMBTON QUAY

HILL

PARLIAMENT

VICTORIA

FEATHERSTON

HARRIS

POST OFFICE
SQUARE

CUSTOMHOUSE QUAY

BALLANCE

STOUT

LAMBTON QUAY

CENOTAPH

WHITMORE

BUNNY

MOLESWORTH

MULGRAVE

Wellington
Harbour

CENTRAL CITY
1. Perretts Corner
2. St George Hotel
3. Thomas killings
4. Clifton carpark toilets
5. NZ Sports Foundation HQ (1992)
6. Edward Gibbon Wakefield's home
7. The Balcony night club
8. Colin Moyle's late-night encounter
9. Charge of the Cossacks

10. Battle of Featherston Street
11. Public Trust offices
12. Old Public Trust Office building
13. 1932 Depression riot
14. Battle of Molesworth Street
15. Parliament: Larnach's suicide
16. The Thistle Inn
17. Old St Paul's
18. Disgrace of an Auditor General
19. Death by duel Sydney St West

44

3.
Central city

1. Perretts Corner, corner Willis & Manners Streets

Perretts Corner is forever tainted by the unprovoked stabbing of a young accountancy student in broad daylight on 14 April 1980.

Miles Macfarlane, the 20-year-old son of Lion Breweries managing director John Macfarlane, was walking down Willis Street, along with shoppers and people finishing work, when the attack occurred. He had just passed the Perretts Corner shopping complex when an unshaven man, who had been following, pulled out a long kitchen knife from a magazine and plunged it into his side. Bewildered bystanders assumed the stabbing was play-acting and few bothered to stop. The knifeman walked around the corner into Manners Street, the blade, dripping with blood, still in his hand. Macfarlane died shortly afterwards at hospital.

The killer, grabbed by police in Manners Street, was Arthur Ball, a 42-year-old unemployed chef and paranoid schizophrenic. This event was later commemorated by the pop group the Mockers in their song 'Murder in Manners Street.'

2. St George Hotel, 1 Boulcott Street

The famous Wellington hotel, now a student hostel, was the scene of the killing of an elderly homosexual on 5 June 1970. Seeward MacGregor, 67, worked there as a steward and met his nemesis there ~ 17-year-old Michael Boyle, who stabbed MacGregor to death during a frenzied attack with a serrated peeling knife. Boyle has since reformed and gone on to be twice runner-up as Wellingtonian of the Year, for his work with troubled youth.

Boyle, who already had a track record of robbing homosexual suitors, met MacGregor at the St George's Seven Seas bar. They then went to the Brunswick Hotel on Upper Willis Street (now demolished) before heading back to MacGregor's upstairs flat on The Terrace. A next-door neighbour found the perforated body at the flat the next morning.

Boyle claimed MacGregor had provoked the attack with his homosexual advances. He had been peeling an apple with the murder weapon when MacGregor tried to kiss him and stroke his thigh. He lost control.

His defence looked shaky from the start. A witness claimed they had slept together and that Boyle didn't have any problems with homosexual contact. And for someone who claimed he had 'lost it' in a moment of violent rage, he was calm enough to rob MacGregor's flat and even try to hack off one of his victim's fingers in an attempt to remove a ring. He was seen trying to sell some of MacGregor's possessions within an hour of the killing.

Released in 1981, he has since changed his name to Micheal Avanti, earning praise for his work with schools to convince teenagers of the perils of a life of crime.

Franconia House, formerly the Invincible Building on The Terrace.

3. Thomas killings ~ 136 The Terrace

Look for a pale yellow, art deco-style building across the road from the James Cook Hotel. It's called Franconia House these days ~ its original name from the 1930s. It was the Invincible Building in 1994 ~ a name forever linked with a double murder and one of the most intriguing court cases in New Zealand's legal history.

From across the street you can see through the fishbowl windows into the third floor ~ the location of Invincible Life Assurance in 1994. The family-owned company was run by 68-year-old Eugene Thomas and his handsome son Gene, 30, a former model. Ambulance staff and police found their bodies on the evening of 16 February 1994 ~ Gene lying face-up in a pool of blood in the foyer, Eugene slumped across the head of the boardroom table.

46

Just a short distance from here some four months later, on 23 June, police arrested 48-year-old antique dealer John Barlow for the execution-style murders as he was walking down The Terrace to see his lawyer.

A cleaner and his teenage son were first to spot the murderer's handiwork ~ spying Gene's body about 6.30pm from a window in the building's old-fashioned lift. Eugene was discovered later when a Telecom worker in an office across the road alerted police that he could see a body leaning on the boardroom table.

Both victims were shot twice with a silenced .32 calibre pistol. The first bullet to hit Gene punched through his hand, ricocheting into the boardroom table. The killer then followed him out to reception area, fatally shooting him in the face. Eugene had two bullet wounds in his head. The pathologist's report said the gun had been pressed against the side of his skull when the first shot was fired. Surprisingly, that bullet didn't kill him. He was reaching for the telephone to dial for help when the killer fired the fatal shot into the back of his head. The phone was still in his hand when police arrived.

The killings looked like a professional hit. There were even rumours of a Mafia link, although they were quickly dispelled. The Thomases' loan and insurance business suggested a more obvious motive. They had made enemies over the years ~ loan repayments forcing at least a couple of clients into bankruptcy.

John Barlow was at the top of the suspect list from an early stage, despite the fact he seemed an unlikely murderer ~ middle-class, happily married, an ex-insurance company manager. Diary records showed the Thomases had been due to meet with Barlow on the day of the murders. Eugene's desk diary page was missing ~ ripped out from the book. But if it was Barlow who did the ripping, he overlooked the Thomases' pocket diaries and Gene's desk diary, all of which confirmed the appointment.

A search of Barlow's home two days after the murders turned up damning evidence ~ a receipt for the Happy Valley rubbish dump, dated the morning after the killings. A police search of the tip unearthed a Czechoslovakian CZ27 pistol, a home-made silencer and some rare .32 Geco ammunition wrapped in separate bundles of newspaper. Barlow's fingerprints were found on the newspaper. It was questionable whether the pistol was the murder weapon, as its barrel was .22 calibre, not .32. The prosecution argued Barlow had changed the barrels before dumping the gun. One of the features of the World War II vintage pistol was that it accepted barrels of either calibre.

The prosecution's case was shaky on motive. Barlow had been friendly with the Thomases and had placed an $80,000 superannuation fund with their company. He had financial problems and had borrowed some $75,000 against the fund, which he couldn't cash up until retirement age. A memo from Gene suggested Barlow was not very happy with the arrangement in which shortfall between the interest on the fund and the interest on the loan was made up by reducing his superannuation deposit. There was no evidence, however, to suggest the superannuation issues were raised at his meeting with the Thomases. Barlow himself claimed the meeting was to bounce ideas around about a new mortgage product, and that the shootings happened after he had left the building.

The absence of clear motive and long drawn-out arguments about the forensic evidence made it tough for the jury members to decide Barlow's guilt. It took three trials to get a conviction – the first two ending with hung juries. Finally, after 27 hours in deliberation, the jury at the third trial found Barlow guilty on 21 November 1995. Barlow, who had been calm throughout the trials, lost his cool when the jury passed its verdict, demanding they be polled to see if the decision was unanimous. It was.

Barlow was sentenced to life imprisonment with a non-parole period of 14 years. In 1996 the Court of Appeal ruled that the convictions should stand. That year he was moved from Mt Crawford, Wellington's medium-security prison, to the Paremoremo maximum-security jail, despite protests from the Barlow family.

The Thomas family ended its formal association with 136 The Terrace in 2000 when Martin Thomas, Gene's brother, sold the former apartment building to a group of local investors to lease as office space. Its linkage with the Thomas name, of course, remains.

4.   Clifton carpark toilets

The public toilets in the Clifton carpark, off The Terrace, are a gay cruising area that has been the target of police raids in recent years. A swoop in March 2000, sparked by public complaints, snared 11 people, including two businessmen, using the loos for sex. The men were charged with offences ranging from indecent acts in a public place to offensive behaviour. They were also issued with trespass notices banning them from using council toilets.

The carpark loos had made headlines earlier that year after a US-based gay website identified them as one of Wellington's best and busiest cruising spots ~ particularly for meeting homosexual office workers and students. The list also included toilets in Central Park, the Botanic Gardens (next to the glass house), the Lower Hutt Town Hall carpark and on an interisland ferry (listed as a former 'cruising site of the week').

Wellington City Council, following the revelations, talked tough about getting rid of the cruising trade from its public toilets, citing plans to replace single-sex loos with multi-gender ones ~ which, according to the council, are less attractive to gay men and tend to be less grubby.

A favourite beat, near Clifton Terrace.

5. NZ Sports Foundation HQ (1992) ~ St John House, 114 The Terrace

Keith Hancox ruled the Sports Foundation from offices in this building (then called Dalmuir House) before losing his empire, his job and his reputation in 1992 for ripping off the sports funding body for more than $1 million.

The former record-breaking New Zealand swimmer faced 482 charges of theft for a spending spree between 1987 and 1992, including flying his family first-class to Britain to watch the Rugby World Cup in 1991 and funding a luxury launch and holiday home on the shores of Lake Tarawera. He used a National Bank Visa card to withdraw cash from money machines, drawing out the maximum each time to pay for his lavish lifestyle, and distorting accounts to hide the fraud ~ in some cases delaying payments to sporting bodies. The theft took place despite a hefty salary of about $180,000 a year. He was sprung after a casual comment to the chief of the Serious Fraud Office at a

49

Heading for the Hall of Infamy: Keith Hancox.
Dominion Post collection

social function. He received a four-year prison sentence on 14 August 1992 and was later dumped from the Sports Hall of Fame, of which he had been both an inductee and an executive director.

6. Edward Gibbon Wakefield's home ~ 90 The Terrace

A plaque commemorates the home where the brains behind the colonial settlement of Wellington spent his final decade ~ depressed and withdrawn from the world. Wakefield's home is long gone, but the significance of the site is recognised by Wakefield House ~ the name of the office building that now occupies the area.

Go to the library if you want to find his theories or the history of the New Zealand Company. The interest for this guide is Wakefield's reputation as a disgraced scoundrel. He came up with his views on colonisation while in Newgate prison (England) for bankruptcy and kidnapping ~ the latter for trying to elope with a young heiress called Ellen Turner. He was also an amateur hypnotist who delighted in inducing frothing fits from people as a party trick. He died bitter and poor in 1862.

His brother William, who arrived in town with an advance party of settlers in 1839, also spent time in prison for the abduction of Turner. He had a reputation for ruthlessness and vindictiveness, and once fought city father Isaac Featherston in a pistol duel in Newtown (see page 65). William, who collapsed

EDWARD GIBBON WAKEFIELD
DIED MAY 16TH 1862
AGED 66 YEARS

A FOUNDER OF THE COLONIES OF NEW ZEALAND
AND SOUTH AUSTRALIA.
AUTHOR OF THE SYSTEM OF COLONISATION
WHICH BEARS HIS NAME. PERSONAL ADVISER TO LORD DURHAM,
GOVERNOR-GENERAL OF CANADA, 1838.
ELECTED TO THE CANADIAN LOWER HOUSE OF ASSEMBLY IN 1842.
FOUNDED NEW ZEALAND ASSOCIATION
AND NEW ZEALAND LAND COMPANY.
ORGANIZED PRELIMINARY EXPEDITION TO
ESTABLISH SETTLEMENTS.
ARRIVED IN NEW ZEALAND IN 1853
AND ELECTED MEMBER OF PROVINCIAL COUNCIL
OF WELLINGTON AND OF THE GENERAL ASSEMBLY.

THE UTMOST HAPPINESS GOD VOUCHSAFES TO MAN
ON EARTH - THE REALIZATION OF HIS OWN IDEA.
E.G.W.

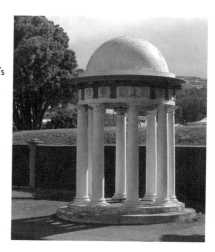

Edward Gibbon Wakefield's grave in Bolton Street Cemetery, and William Wakefield's Grecian-style memorial at the Basin Reserve.

and died leaving a Turkish bath house in 1848, is remembered by a run-down Grecian-style memorial on the eastern side of the Basin Reserve.

7. The Balcony night club ~ corner Victoria & Harris Streets

The Wellington Public Library now occupies the site of Carmen's Balcony nightclub ~ probably the second-most famous of the high-profile transsexual's late-night entertainment venues (*see* Red Light District, No 7, for background on her International Coffee Lounge).

Carmen decided to add a cabaret nightspot to her growing empire in the early 1970s. The entertainment included drag queens and strippers of all persuasions, along with more traditional cabaret acts ~ The Red Mole satirical group among them. Carmen presided over the show, usually glammed up like a whorehouse madam. The nightclub attracted national media attention in the wake of the Colin Moyle affair (*see* No 8) in 1975.

8. Colin Moyle's late-night encounter ~ Harris Street

A plainclothes police officer patrolling the area near The Balcony nightclub was walking down Harris Street about 11pm on 17 June 1975 when a car started following him. Pulling up next to the young officer, the driver asked him to hop inside. The man behind the wheel turned out to be Colin Moyle, Labour MP for Mangere and Minister of Agriculture and Fisheries. The incident occurred close to the old library bogs in Mercer Street (destroyed to make way for the new library in the early 1990s) ~ a well-known cruising area for gay men. Homosexual sex was illegal back then, and the incident went on, courtesy of Rob Muldoon's malicious manipulation, to cause an uproar in Parliament, ending with Moyle's resignation.

Discovering his passenger was a cop, Moyle said he thought the officer was a friend for whom he was waiting to come out of the library ~ even though the library had closed two hours earlier. The officer let him go. Voluntarily going back to the police station the next morning, he changed his story, saying he had arranged a meeting with a homosexual in order to research a bill that was due to appear shortly before

Colin Moyle, MP for Mangere, and his wife Millicent, 5 November 1976.
Alexander Turnbull Library
Dominion Post collection
Obits-Moyle-01

52

Parliament. The police told him that the matter wouldn't be taken any further.

Much to the horror of Moyle and the Labour Party the affair resurfaced a year later during a fiery debate in Parliament. Newly elected prime minister Rob Muldoon, wishing to deflect attention from a question by Moyle about dodgy dealings by his old accountancy firm, made a reference to the member of Mangere being picked up for homosexual activity. Moyle gave a statement to Parliament the next day, saying he had spoken to a man he suspected of burglary ~ contradicting what he had told police a year earlier.

An inquiry was launched, headed by retired Court of Appeal president Sir Alfred North. North concluded that Moyle couldn't justify what he had said in the House, prompting the MP's resignation. But that wasn't the end of the matter. There was criticism that North exceeded his powers on constitutional grounds. And there were demands that the government release the evidence gathered by the inquiry. It didn't.

The scandal didn't destroy Moyle's political career. He returned to Parliament in 1981 in the Hunua seat, and he later became Minister of Agriculture and Fisheries again in the fourth Labour government (1984-90).

Muldoon ~ the perpetrator of the affair ~ may well have been its ultimate victim. Moyle's resignation resulted in a by-election in Mangere, bringing David Lange into Parliament, who went on to lead Labour to victory against National in 1984.

9. Charge of the Cossacks ~ Post Office Square

Mounted special police charged a crowd of strikers and onlookers here on 30 October 1913, batoning women, children and anyone else who got in the way of their flailing clubs.

The charge was one of the nastier encounters between police and striking watersiders in 1913. Its brutality earned the 'specials' the nickname 'Massey's Cossacks', after the then prime minister. And it hardened union opposition to the government to the extent that, for a while at least, civil war was on the cards.

The violence had been brewing since the watersiders went on strike on 22 October over shipowners' refusal to pay travelling money to men working on the Evan's Bay patent slip. They returned to work to find their jobs taken by other men ~ 'scabs'. Scuffles erupted

as the watersiders tried to stop the free labour from working the ships, prompting the police to recruit special constables from the countryside. The specials, many of them farmers desperate to see their perishable produce shipped out, quickly gained a reputation for indiscriminate use of force and were hated by the strikers and regular police alike.

The Post Office Square charge was partly retaliation by the specials after the strikers had forced them to flee Waterloo Quay. Some of the crowd tried to pull the riders from their horses, but were batoned back. There were reports of gunfire, but no one was hit. An angry mob chased one special constable up Lambton Quay. He ducked into the Whitcombe & Tombs bookshop, now Whitcoulls, and jumped out a back window. The mob outside ripped up wooden blocks from the road and started throwing them at the shop ~ knocking out a policeman in the process. The crowd cleared when a shop assistant grabbed an unloaded pistol from the strong room, brandishing it at the strikers.

'Massey's Cossacks': Special constables assembled at Mount Cook Barracks during the 1913 waterfront strike.
Alexander Turnbull Library F96909 1/2

As a show of government force, armed soldiers took to parading around Wellington with a Gatling gun and uncovered bayonets. The strikers held the upper hand for a while, restricting work on the waterfront to King's Wharf ~ the only wharf serviced by a railway. The strike, however, petered out in early December ~ largely due to disunity in union movement that saw a lukewarm response to the United Federation of Labour's call for a general strike.

10. Battle of Featherston Street ~ corner Featherston & Stout Streets

Special constables repeatedly charged waterside strikers and their supporters at the intersection on 5 November 1913 (No 8, for background on the strike).

The strikers were trying to stop the loading of racehorses onto a steamer at the Railway Wharf (which was across the road from the current Wellington Station), despite permission from the strike committee for the loading to proceed. The horses were bound for a New Zealand Cup meeting in Christchurch.

Anticipating trouble, a column of nearly 1000 mounted specials left the camp at Mt Cook to provide a guard. They started getting pelted with stones at the

corner of Willis Street and Ghuznee Street. The hail of missiles become stronger as the column passed each intersection on the way down Featherston Street. It had become a blizzard by the time it reached Stout Street, with the rearguard under attack from flying scrap iron, bottles, bolts and broken bricks. Deciding to retaliate, the rear ranks turned into Stout Street and galloped into the mob with swinging batons. The mob scattered in all directions, but quickly reformed, resulting in more charges.

The prolonged fighting caused about 50 injuries ~ many of them severe head gashes from the missiles. Nurses treated the wounded on the grass outside the old railway offices near the corner. Detectives mingling in the crowd made eight arrests, including a tramway conductor in full uniform.

As soon as the fighting died down, the crowd surged into Waterloo Quay to hear addresses by the strike leaders from a loading platform. Bob Semple ~

then a United Federation of Labour organiser, later a cabinet minister in the first Labour government ~ gave a long and contradictory harangue that left the crowd unclear of his support. He appealed that the strikers to "do no act which would allow the authorities an excuse to retaliate". The crowd dispersed as darkness fell, unsuccessful in its attempt to stop the loading of the racehorses.

11. Public Trust offices ~ 117 Lambton Quay

The Public Trust offices in Lambton Quay were the workplace of Norrie Triggs ~ a 51-year-old computer programmer found bashed to death at his bedsit in Chartwell, near Crofton Downs, in February 1994. His murder remains unsolved.

A curious thing about Triggs was that police first thought they were investigating the killing of a quiet loner. People who knew him assumed he was a homosexual. Far from it; the investigation showed Triggs to be something of a Lothario, despite his plain looks. He was nicknamed 'The Moth', because he liked to flit around women. Police estimated he had bedded as many as 900 over 30 years.

Norrie's bedroom habits may have been his undoing. Forensic evidence showed he had had sex just before his beating. The death blow may very well have come from the woman involved. Police have identified a woman as the prime suspect, but there has never been enough evidence to make an arrest.

12. Old Public Trust building ~ 131-135 Lambton Quay

The classic baroque-styled building was home to the Public Trust in 1929, and it was where another 'Norrie' (actually Norris ~ Norris Davey) was working as a lawyer at the time of his arrest for a homosexual tryst with a Christchurch artist. He was caught in the act during a police raid on a local boarding house. Davey received a suspended sentence. He later changed his name to Frank Sargeson, becoming one of New Zealand's best-known writers.

13. 1932 Depression riot ~ Cenotaph, Lambton Quay

The Cenotaph, on 10 May 1932, was the starting point for Wellington's biggest and most destructive riot of the Depression years.

An angry crowd of 5000 had gathered outside the gates of Parliament to pressure the government to rescind its changes to the relief work scheme. (The Unemployment Board had announced in April it would be cutting payments and that it would force single unemployed men to leave the city for work camps in the countryside).

Many of the crowd were members of the Unemployed Workers Union, and had gathered at the Basin Reserve earlier that morning and voted to strike the relief scheme.

Public Trust building, Lambton Quay.

Expecting public works minister Gordon Coates to front up, the crowd waited all afternoon – their anger slowly coming to a boil when Coates didn't show. Soon after dark, union delegates returned from a meeting with government officials to address the crowd. They said Coates had made a small concession for married relief workers, but had effectively promised nothing. (One delegate later alleged that Coates, reminiscent of Marie Antoinette, had said "the hungry could eat grass".)

The news sparked a violent response. "Up the town" was the cry (or "Down the town", depending on which account you read). About 50 demonstrators set off up Lambton Quay, overturning an Indian fruit cart and stopping to pick up the fruit and bits of wooden boxes to use as missiles and clubs. Followed by a baying crowd, they charged up the quay and Willis Street, smashing windows and overturning cars as they went.

The papers later reported damage all the way to the James Smith building in lower Cuba Street.

The police were caught wrong-footed and were unable to stop the initial charge. They later regrouped and waded into the rioters with batons outside the Whitcombe & Tombs building (now Whitcoulls); but all that did was drive the crowd into Featherston Street. It took a police cordon along Manners Street at around 7pm to finally gain control. The riot resulted in more than £2000 of damage, including the cost of some 170 smashed windows. There were 23 arrests. The Kirkcaldie & Stains Building in Lambton Quay was worst hit – losing eleven large display windows.

The relief workers strike lasted until 21 May, collapsing without achieving any concessions from the government, or even a statement from Gordon Coates.

The Cenotaph: starting point for Wellington's worst Depression riot.

14. Battle of Molesworth Street

Molesworth Street was the scene of one of the defining moments of the 1981 clashes between police and anti-Springbok tour demonstrators. It was the first time the police had come out swinging their long batons at the protestors – a tipping point for the violent confrontations that were to follow for the remainder of the tour.

Wellington police had decided to adopt hard-line tactics following two events on 25 July. The first was the cancellation of the game between the South Africans and Waikato after protesters invaded the field and reports that a pilot in a stolen aircraft was planning to crash into the grandstand. On the same day some 1500 protestors had blocked the Wellington motorway for four hours.

The Molesworth Street showdown took place four days later on 29 July when protesters gathered in Parliament grounds around 5pm with the intention of marching on the South African consul's residence,

then based on the other side of the motorway in Wadestown. Determined not to see a repeat of the previous motorway blockage, the police tried to contain the demonstration in the grounds. The protestors ignored police requests and moved out of Parliament's lower gates into Molesworth Street. Police officers linked arms to form a cordon, but found themselves getting pushed up the street towards a second line of officers. Worried the protestors were going to break through, the second line of cops lurched forward, punching and kicking the exposed protestors. A baton charge followed. Some 20 to 30 protestors were hit, many repeatedly.

Shocked by the ferocity of the police, the marchers turned around and headed back to the Cenotaph, then along Lambton Quay. Some of the demonstrators gathered angrily in Waring Taylor Street. Police feared they would storm the nearby Central Police Station, but things calmed down fairly quickly and the protestors went home.

The great fire at the Parliamentary Buildings, 1907.

The charge tainted the police in the eyes of many opponents of the tour; they were seen as supporting the tour, rather than neutral defenders of the law. It also led to a change of tactics for the demonstrators. They steered away from large-scale protests, preferring instead highly mobile squads intended to stretch police resources to breaking point.

Historians regard the events of that day and that of the rest of the tour as the peak of the New Zealand's protest movement's revolt against Rob Muldoon's conservative and populist politics ~ a movement that had been gathering pace since the early 1970s.

15. Larnach's suicide ~ old Parliament building site

It was inside Committee Room 'J' above the lobby of the old Parliament building that William Larnach ended his political career with a bullet to the head. William Larnach had arrived in New Zealand in 1867, aged 34, with his wife and four children. He became a successful banker, businessman, land speculator and a politician. He helped pioneer the Otago dairy industry and later the frozen meat trade. In 1880, with two more daughters, his Dunedin castle finished and his fortune at its peak, his wife Eliza died suddenly and his life became a series of catastrophes. He lost two fortunes, a second wife also died, his children proved troublesome and with his financial downturns many of his friends disappeared.

His financial position on the mend, he married Constance de Bathe Brandon, 22 years his junior.

Some of his children, fearful she might inherit the family money, made her life miserable. Years later a final catastrophe came when he discovered his son Douglas was cuckolding him with Constance. He received a letter through the parliamentary post that seemed to visibly upset him. He posted a reply, then entered the committee room. A shot was heard. And, after bashing down the door, officials found Larnach dead in the chairman's seat, with a revolver in his hand and a bullet in his left temple.

Neither letter has ever been traced. Following his death both Douglas and Constance were disinherited. Constance returned to Wellington and never remarried.

A fire destroyed the wooden building in 1907. In its place is the grand Edwardian structure that was constructed from Takaka marble and has housed New Zealand's Parliament since 1922.

16. The Thistle Inn ~ 3 Mulgrave Street

The Thistle Inn is the city's oldest pub. Condemned by some as a dump (before the recent refurbishment), the inn is one of the last vestiges of Wellington's drunken and lawless frontier days. Early Wellington was far from the idyllic paradise portrayed by the New Zealand Company to attract settlers. The small, mostly male, population was well served by hotels and grog shops along the waterfront ~ some 20 for a population of only 2000 by 1843. Best-known was Dicky Barrett's, owned by one of the more interesting characters of early Wellington. Its most popular incarnation was on the site of the High Court in Molesworth Street. Not surprisingly, drunkenness, brawling and dalliance with prostitutes were popular pastimes, particularly among the whalers and sailors. The streets and beaches were often strewn with broken glass.

The Thistle dates to 1840, although most of its timbers are from 1866, when it was rebuilt after a fire. It used to be right next to the shoreline, convenient for drinkers arriving by boat, before a series of land reclamations pushed it back from the sea. The story goes that Te Rauparaha, Ngati Toa chief, once landed his canoe outside the tavern and went in for some rum. No one had the nerve to ask him to pay.

The inn also features in an unpublished lesbian story by Wellington writer Katherine Mansfield. The story created a scandal for her family when she tried to get it typed up, leading to pressure on her to leave the country, which she duly did.

Opposite: Thorndon Quay and Mulgrave
Street in 1866, showing the Thistle Inn (the first
building on the rise) and St Paul's Church.
Alexander Turnbull Library F52971 1/2

17. Old St Paul's ~ 34 Mulgrave Street

Old St Paul's was the site of public stocks before the building of the colonial gothic church in 1865. It was used for drying out the local drunks ~ some the result of a night on the town at the Thistle Inn (*see* No 16).

18. Disgrace of an Auditor General, 48 Mulgrave Street

The Audit Office's headquarters in Mulgrave Street was the workplace of convicted fraudster Jeff Chapman from 1992 to 1994.

A short, pushy man who had previously been Society of Accountants president, Chapman was Auditor General ~ the government's top financial watchdog. That didn't stop him ripping off his employer, an act that set off constitutional alarm bells and rocked the accountancy world.

The Audit Office found Chapman's fingers in the till in 1994. His daughter was working for the office at time.

Officials called her in to say her father would be leaving in disgrace. The Accident Compensation Corporation ~ where Chapman had earned a reputation for lavish spending during his seven years as managing director ~ unearthed further fraud.

His personal finances in a mess, he stole to meet overdue mortgage payments and other outstanding bills. The money also went to fund his high living ~ including first-class travel and expensive hotels.

Chapman was convicted on ten charges of using documents with intent to defraud involving $54,594 in February 1997 and later given a six-month prison sentence. The Court of Appeal overturned that sentence a couple of months later, increasing it to 18 months, saying the original sentence didn't reflect the responsibilities of Chapman's position and the breach of trust involved.

The Audit Office's headquarters in Mulgrave Street.

19. Death by duel

The first — and one of the few — deaths in New Zealand from duelling happened in Wellington at Sydney Street Gully, near the present day Anderson Park, in 1844. The protagonists were solicitor Hugh Ross, who had defended one AE McDonough in a land claim, and William Brewer, a barrister for the losing party. An upset arose from the decision in the case and the lawyers' conduct and a challenge was issued. The duel took place on 26 February. Ross's second was Major David Durie (later to make a mark in Wanganui). Brewer fired into the air; Ross hit him in the groin and he died a week later. Some years later McDonough, beset with gambling problems, killed himself with one of the duelling pistols.

Wellington's other renowned duel involved

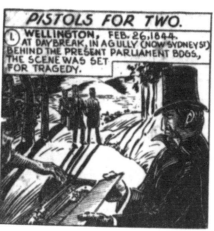

An excerpt from Ross Gore's cartoon in the *Evening Post*.

two men immortalised in street names: hot-tempered Dr Isaac Featherston and Colonel William Wakefield, who fought to resolve long-standing political and social animosity. Featherston, as editor of the Wellington *Independent*, was repeatedly critical of the activities of Wakefield's New Zealand Land Company. In the small town that Wellington was at the time there were social repercussions, and tension between the men finally culminated in a duel in Newtown, which at the time was very much hinterland. Featherston fired first and missed; Wakefield fired into the air, saying later that he had not wanted to kill a man with seven daughters. The two adversaries made amends and Featherston continued to act as Wakefield's doctor.

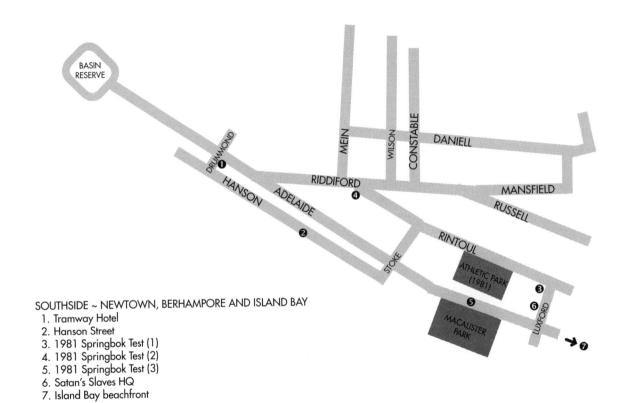

SOUTHSIDE ~ NEWTOWN, BERHAMPORE AND ISLAND BAY
1. Tramway Hotel
2. Hanson Street
3. 1981 Springbok Test (1)
4. 1981 Springbok Test (2)
5. 1981 Springbok Test (3)
6. Satan's Slaves HQ
7. Island Bay beachfront

4.
Southside ~ Newtown, Berhampore and Island Bay

1.   Tramway Hotel ~ 114 Adelaide Road

Gang rivalry at this once coarse and violent Newtown watering hole exploded in August 1981 ~ resulting in the fatal beating of a Mongrel Mob leader as he ran for his life down Adelaide Road.

The local Mongrel Mob headquarters was based down the road at Brown Street (next to the BP station) in 1981. Mob members drank at the Tramway, as did members of the Eastern Suburbs Rugby League Club ~ which had links to Black Power. The team had its clubrooms at the pub.

Tension increased after the league players recruited a mobster to play for them. On 14 August it reached snapping point after the team captain's car was damaged in the carpark. Club members, armed with baseball bats and fence palings, raided the Mongrel Mob house. The gang beat them back.

'If walls could talk' ~ now gentrified, the Tramways has had a turbulent past.

At dawn next day the league players made another attack, this time equipped with baseball bats, slashers and axe handles. The gang was expecting them. Leader Lester Epps had stationed himself in an old ambulance outside the house to keep watch. Unfortunately for him he fell asleep, giving the league players the element

67

of surprise. They battered their way into the house, beating up all they encountered.

Epps awoke to the sound of the attackers smashing in the ambulance windows. He tried to escape by releasing the handbrake and rolling down Brown Street. Near the bottom he tried to flee on foot, turning right into Adelaide Road. The fit league players easily caught him, laying into him with their weapons close to the Basin Reserve. Epps never recovered from his head injuries. His life support system was turned off three days later.

None of the league players was tried for murder, as there was uncertainty about who had landed the fatal blow. Fourteen members of the club were found guilty of manslaughter, each receiving 18 months imprisonment.

The Tramway cleaned up its act under the ownership of Wellington strip-club baron Brian Le Gros in the 1990s. The gangs are no longer there in force and the building has been awarded heritage status. The bar has undergone facelifts and name changes since Epps' murder. Its name recently reverted back to the original Tramway Hotel.

2.   Hanson Street

Hanson Street has a criminal reputation that the ongoing gentrification of Berhampore and Newtown has yet to cleanse.

The Highway 61 motorcycle gang was based in a derelict warehouse near the corner of Drummond Street for many years, before moving to Maupuia industrial zone in the late 1990s. Schoolkids used to rate the headquarters as a sure bet for buying cannabis, despite regular police surveillance and raids.

The street was also once home to Trevor Rupe, who went on to become Carmen, Wellington's most famous transsexual. Working down the road at the Wellington hospital by day and experimenting with drag by night, Rupe lived across the road from the old Alexandra maternity home (28A Hanson Street), from where young fathers were a popular score for Rupe and her friends' gay sex sessions at the house. Police charged Rupe with brothel keeping at the Hanson Street address in 1961 after a prostitute moved into the house. She spent the winter of that year in Mt Crawford, enjoying the male company and her notoriety as the only whorehouse madam in the men-only prison.

3. 1981 Springbok Test (1) ~ corner Luxford & Rintoul Streets

There was blood on the streets of this intersection after one of the most violent altercations between police and protestors during the 1981 Springboks tour.

It was the day of the Wellington test match ~ 29 August. COST (Citizens Opposed to the Springbok Tour), the local anti-tour group, was determined to disrupt the game, largely by using seated protestors to block street intersections around Athletic Park, then Wellington's international rugby ground, now the site of a residential development.

Part of the plan was to assault the park directly. COST's 'Brown Section' set off running through private premises as soon as the game started, aiming to pull down the wire fences on the perimeter. They managed to cut a small hole through one of the fences before police repelled them, herding them back to the Luxford/Rintoul intersection.

The violence started when the police line manning the intersection had to open to let the failed raiding party through from behind. A huge crowd of protesters in front of the police started to move forward. Fearing a stampede, the police's Red Squad let rip with their long batons. Protestors retaliated with missiles ~ rubbish bin lids, stones and, allegedly, acid bombs.

COST later complained the police were out of control, and even the police conceded that some of the head injuries sustained by the protestors were over the top. An Ombudsman's report backed the police on the whole, but criticised them for failing to make clear what they intended to do with the Brown Section members. It also commented that some individual officers had gone too far with their use of force. COST was unsuccessful with its call for a government inquiry.

4. 1981 Springbok Test (2) ~ corner Rintoul & Riddiford Streets

The intersection saw police use a wedge formation to plough a path for rugby spectators through a crowd of seated anti-tour demonstrators attempting to block access to Athletic Park ~ venue for one of the 1981 test matches. There were numerous arrests, and many protestors suffered baton injuries in the push, or were hurt when they were forced through broken glass shop windows by the police.

5. 1981 Springbok Test (3) ~ Macalister Park, Adelaide Road

Police and anti-tour protestors stood off face-to-face at Macalister Park in 1981 ~ just across the road from Athletic Park, the venue for the second test match of the series between the All Blacks and the Springboks. The protesters came up against the police after using grappling hooks to tear down a line of barbed wire. The standoff didn't escalate into a riot, but ~ fearful that rugby supporters would take to the crowd with their fists once the game was over ~ the police kept the gates of Athletic Park closed until they could escort the protestors back to the central city. The walk back to the city took the protestors back pass the Caledonian Hotel at the bottom of Adelaide Road. During their march up to park earlier that day they had been pelted with glasses and glass jugs from tour supporters drinking at the hotel.

Athletic Park closed in 1999 and is now the site of a huge housing development. The sportsgrounds of Macalister Park remain pretty much as they were in 1981, as does the Caledonian Hotel.

6. Satan's Slaves HQ ~ 10A Luxford Street

A high concrete wall and steel grille gate barricade the headquarters of motorcycle gang Satan's Slaves from the street. There was a metal swastika welded to the gate for a month or so in 1995. The gang removed it after complaints from neighbours and the threat of prosecution from the Wellington City Council.

Police regard the Slaves as one of the most violent gangs in the lower North Island. The gang hasn't been shy in making its presence felt to its Luxford Street neighbours since moving into the property in 1986. Noise complaints about loud parties over the years fill a large dossier at the council archives. Luxford Street has been the scene of running battles between police and the gang when officers have shown up to quieten things down. The Armed Offenders Squad has made at least a couple of visits, and the property was the scene of a gang rape in the late 1980s.

The gang's been pretty quiet for a while, but a few years ago it was seldom out of the news ~ mostly for drug offences. Police targeted the gang and its associates in a big drug bust called Operation Wand in 1994. The sting resulted in more than 30 arrests among Satan's Slaves members. The following year a

High Court judge accused the gang of being more concerned with drug dealing than motorcycles when he sentenced patch member Mark Albon, a former president, for organising New Zealand's largest known illegal importation of amphetamine.

The gang attracted more headlines and a major blow to its macho pride in late 1996 when two Samoan newspaper boys fought off Slaves armed with pool cues and other weapons around the corner in nearby Herald Street. The fight started after the two teenagers, delivering the *Contact* newspaper, upset a dog outside the gang's headquarters. Three gang members used a car to chase the teens, who armed themselves with fence posts when they saw them coming. When the Slaves jumped out and swung their weapons one of the boys whacked the nearest attacker on his head, shattering his skull and squirting blood over the road in full view of pre-school children and their parents at a nearby learning centre. The Slave survived, but suffered brain damage and had to have a metal plate inserted to repair his badly fractured skull. Police accepted the paperboys had acted in self-defence and did not lay charges.

The Slaves have been a little quieter since the Planning Tribunal issued an interim enforcement in

The Luxford Street headquarters of the Satan's Slaves, 1995.
Alexander Turnbull Library Dominion Post collection 1995/1850/15A

late 1995 that banned loud music and stopped gang members from using the Luxford Street property as clubrooms at night.

The council considered buying the residential Berhampore property in 1996 and helping relocate the Slaves to council-owned land in Rongotai's industrial area. Those plans, much to the relief of the Rongotai ratepayers' association, fell flat.

7.   Island Bay beachfront

Two fishermen spotted the body of John Maltby floating near the beach on 24 September 1961, ending a huge hunt for the man suspected of abducting and murdering Lower Hutt teenager Wendy Mayes. Wendy had gone missing from her parents' home at 167 Whites Line East after answering a newspaper ad looking for calendar models.

Mayes, who the *Evening Post* described as "a most attractive 16-year-old girl", met Maltby at a city coffee bar on 14 September to discuss the calendar deal. Maltby was a Wellington butcher and store owner with a shady past (criminal records in Australia and England). He had recently purchased a modelling business. Four days later, Mayes met Maltby again. She telephoned her mum to say she would be late home, but was never seen again, despite weeks of extensive searching throughout the Wellington region.

Maltby was involved in a scuffle with police outside Anvil House in Wakefield Street a couple of days after Mayes's disappearance. He was brought in for questioning, but released soon after. Under surveillance at his home in Newtown, he eluded police in thick scrub near the house, before apparently drowning himself at Island Bay.

5.
Other infamous city sites

1. Where Dr Sutch met the KGB agent ~ corner Aro Street & Holloway Road

The small park at the top of Aro Street at the entrance to Holloway Road is a landmark for espionage, scandal and cold war paranoia. It is where police and Security Intelligence Service officers watched Dr William Sutch meet with a Russian KGB officer on the rainy evening of 26 September 1974, resulting in New Zealand's first and only prosecution for spying under the Official Secrets Act.

The SIS had been observing Sutch ~ a former high-level public servant ~ for several months. Tipped off about the Holloway Road meeting, SIS officers and police were hiding in the area ~ including inside the Aro Street public toilets ~ with the hope of catching Sutch in the act of passing information to the Russians.

Sutch took them by surprise by arriving in a taxi (he had been expected to walk) at the corner at around 8.30pm. While confusion reigned he made his way along the path towards Entrance Street, stopping near the World War I memorial. It was there he met Russian embassy official Dmitri Razgovorov, who had walked down the path from the opposite direction.

The SIS alleged Sutch handed a package to Razgovorov, who walked back to his diplomatic car and passed it to the driver. Leaving Razgovorov standing on the pavement, the black Mercedes sped off, presumably taking the package back to the Soviet embassy in Messines Road, Karori. An SIS officer ran after Razgovorov, stopping him in Aro Street. Protected by diplomatic immunity, the Russian revealed little when questioned.

A police officer stopped Sutch outside 1 Holloway Road. Sutch claimed he had left the taxi to take a pee and had then walked up Holloway Road to study the area's historical buildings. He planned to walk back down Aro Street to catch another cab to his home.

Sutch agreed to a search of his house the following day. Police found a diary listing times and places for previous meetings with the Russian. He was then

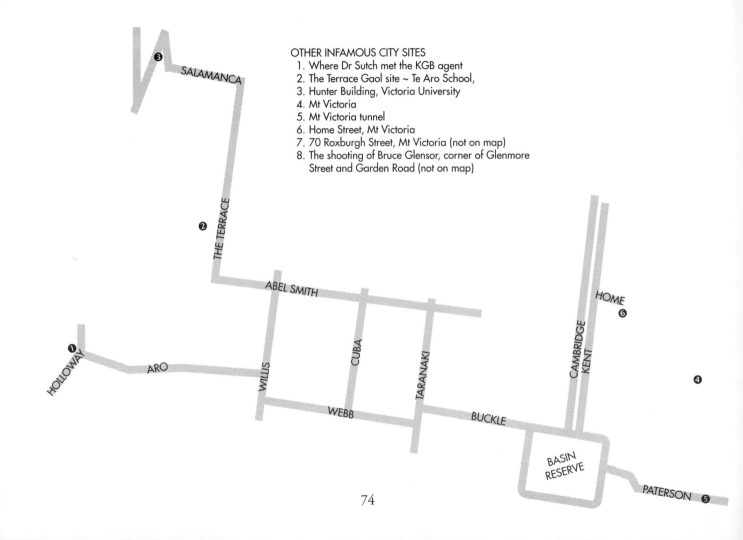

OTHER INFAMOUS CITY SITES
1. Where Dr Sutch met the KGB agent
2. The Terrace Gaol site ~ Te Aro School,
3. Hunter Building, Victoria University
4. Mt Victoria
5. Mt Victoria tunnel
6. Home Street, Mt Victoria
7. 70 Roxburgh Street, Mt Victoria (not on map)
8. The shooting of Bruce Glensor, corner of Glenmore
   Street and Garden Road (not on map)

74

arrested and charged with obtaining information that might be useful to an enemy. Following his arrest, Sutch gave a number of reasons to explain his meetings with the Russian ~ one being that he was interested in Zionism and had sought Razgovorov's views on the subject.

The case went to trial in October. Sutch was found not guilty, largely because the SIS officers hadn't actually seen him pass anything to the diplomat. There was also no evidence presented about what was in the mystery package. Despite the verdict, suspicions lingered about Sutch's Soviet connections. Sutch himself didn't have to worry about the whispers for long. He died of cancer a few months after the trial.

Was he a spy? A Television New Zealand reporter came close to solving the mystery during a visit to Moscow in 2000. A former Chargé d'Affaires at the Soviet embassy confirmed papers had been passed to Razgovorov, but he believed they were relatively innocuous briefing documents prepared by Sutch on political and economic matters. The ex-diplomat, however, was in no doubt that Sutch had been a Russian

The war memorial site in Aro Street where Dr Sutch met the KGB agent.

75

mole for decades. The reporter also tracked down Razgovorov, but he refused to speak. Razgovorov has since died, taking his secrets to the grave.

2. The Terrace Gaol site ~ Te Aro School, south end of The Terrace

Te Aro School stands on the site of the old Terrace Gaol ~ a final abode before the gallows for many of early Wellington's nastiest criminals. The site is accessible from the St John Street steps in Aro Street.

The prison was built in 1852, closing in 1926 when superseded by Mt Crawford Prison on the Miramar Peninsula. The gaol was full for much of its life, many of its inmates coming from the slums that sprang up around Te Aro in the 1860s.

Notorious Newlands baby farmer Daniel Cooper was one of its prisoners, although only briefly ~ he was hanged at the gaol on 16 June 1923. Cooper is reviled second only to Southland's infamous Minnie Dean for his crimes. He was an illegal abortionist who killed and disposed of newborn infants from mothers too far gone in their pregnancies to abort ~ promising the mothers he would find good homes for their kids. He was nabbed after the body of an infant was found at Lyall Bay beach. That death had nothing to do with Cooper, but police decided to dig up his farm at Newlands after an anonymous tip-off. He was charged with the murder of four babies, including two children Cooper had fathered by his housemaid Beatrice Beadle. The trial attracted huge public interest, with crowds queuing outside the court from early in the morning. A gaol warder reported that, on the day of the hanging, Cooper was so terrified they couldn't get his head into the noose. He had to be poked in the eyes to get his head to flick back.

Frenchman Etienne Brocher was another notable prisoner who wound up at the end of a gaol noose. He had stabbed to death an elderly couple in their Petone grocery shop in August 1896. Posing under the name Stephen Bosher at the time of the murders, he had a long criminal history ~ including having been sentenced to serve with the French Foreign Legion in Algiers. He eventually confessed and was hanged on 21 April 1897. The hanging attracted a huge crowd. Prison authorities had to shield the scaffold with tarpaulins when people started climbing the nearby hills to get a view.

The Terrace Gaol, in the right foreground, at the south end of The Terrace,
c.1906. It is now the site of Te Aro School.
Courtesy Terence Hodgson

Archibald Baxter (father of poet James K Baxter) was incarcerated in The Terrace Gaol for refusing to fight in the World War I, then sent to the battlefields of France and tortured in an attempt to get him to fight. His story is graphically told in *We Will Not Cease*, which has been reissued by Cape Catley publishers.

We were marched along, clumping in our clumsy boots, through corridors and doorways, till we came to a hall in the main building, flanked by cells on either side. Here we were each locked in a cell. I had had some experience of cells in the preceding month, but this was infinitely worse than anything I had known. To begin with, the door was always shut with a resounding slam and locked with a great clashing of keys, producing a sense of the inexorableness of the grasp in which one was held. The cell itself, narrow, dank and airless, gave me a feeling of physical oppression. The building was so large, the cell so small, that the walls seemed to be closing in upon one. The window, tiny, high up and closely barred, gave upon a wall; consequently so little light found its way into the cell that it was hardly possible to read at midday. It contained a straw mattress, up-ended against the wall, and blankets folded neatly, a pillow, a stool, a shelf, a tin basin, and a tin chamber-pot. I had not been long in the cell when the door was opened with more clashing of keys and dinner brought round by prisoner orderlies, escorted by a warder. It consisted of stew with vegetables and potatoes, quite wholesome. When we were taken out into the yard a little later, Jack whispered to me: 'Well, the dinner wasn't too bad, anyway. Perhaps things won't be so bad here, after all.'

The exercise yard was surrounded by high brick walls. On the roof was a pagoda-like structure, built to shelter the armed warder, who, from his position, could command the whole of the yard. For the first part of the exercise period the prisoners mingled together and talked indiscriminately amongst themselves; but on a given signal from the warder in charge, they formed into pairs and marched around and round the ring. At the side of the yard stood a row of w.c.s. Anyone wishing to use them - and one was supposed to train oneself to do so at this time - shouted 'Rear!' An interchange of shouts with the warder generally followed, depending on whether there was an unoccupied cubicle or not. In time we became quite accustomed to this public performance.

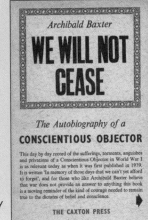

Archibald Baxter
WE WILL NOT CEASE

The Autobiography of a
CONSCIENTIOUS OBJECTOR

This day by day record of the sufferings, torments, anguishes and privations of a Conscientious Objector in World War I is as relevant today as when it was first published in 1939. It is written 'In memory of those days that we can't yet afford to forget', and for those who like Archibald Baxter believe that war does not provide an answer to anything this book is a moving reminder of the kind of courage needed to remain true to the dictates of belief and conscience.

THE CAXTON PRESS

The first NZ edition of Archie Baxter's classic.

Joseph Pawelka cemented his place in New Zealand's criminal history when, after three failed attempts, he finally escaped from The Terrace Gaol in 1911 and was never seen again. The house-breaker had run amok the previous year in the Manawatu after escaping from the Lambton Quay police station. Two people were shot dead in attempts to bring him back to justice ~ one a police sergeant who tackled the escapee when he was running from a house; the other a searcher who, in a tragic case of mistaken identity (he was wearing similar leggings to Pawelka's), collected a bullet from a fellow searcher. Pawelka was eventually caught with two loaded revolvers in a barn near Ashhurst. Tried for the killing of the sergeant, he was found not guilty, but received a whopping 21-year sentence for theft and arson.

The severity of the sentence shocked many, prompting petitions to have it reduced. Pawelka didn't wait for the outcome. He managed to scale the prison wall on his

Joseph Pawelka.

third escape attempt, but was spotted by the wife of a former gaoler. The police found him hiding in a heap of old newspapers in a nearby cottage. When he began to struggle in his handcuffs, the constable pointed his revolver. The watching crowd cried "Shoot!" while Pawelka pleaded for his life.

He was fourth-time lucky. Confined to one of the cells reserved for condemned prisoners, Pawelka was able to lift out the bars of his window. He was last seen by a milkboy heading towards the Botanic Gardens. The bars were found to have been doctored by fellow prisoners who had recently renovated the cell. They were embedded in soap and wood shavings rather than concrete.

3. Hunter Building ~ Victoria University, Kelburn Parade

Victoria University's ivy-swathed Hunter Building is famous for its majestic architecture and for its historical status as the original building on campus. It is infamous for the worst incident of radioactive contamination in New Zealand's history – an incident that university hierarchy covered up for more than 25 years, and one that may have led to the death of a staff member.

The *Sunday Star* newspaper uncovered the building's dark (er... glowing) secret in 1988 when a former laboratory technician from the university's physics department decided to speak to the media to highlight the dangers of experimenting with new technology. He first detected high radiation levels in the department's laboratories, based in the building, in 1961. The Health Department later confirmed hazardous, although not lethal, contamination throughout the department – the worst being in staff offices. One patch of wall was found to be contaminated 300 times above the British safety standard.

The Health Department report came out in July 1963 – too late for physics lecturer Ron Humphrey, 37, who died of leukaemia earlier that year, and whose widow later reached an out-of-court settlement with the university after suing for damages. Ironically, the legal action may have increased the extent to which departmental staff were exposed to radiation.

The varsity locked away evidence for the case – contaminated fittings and furniture – in an upstairs room of the Hunter Building and promptly forgot about them. The vice-chancellor of the day went white when he heard the heavily contaminated material was still in the building some months later.

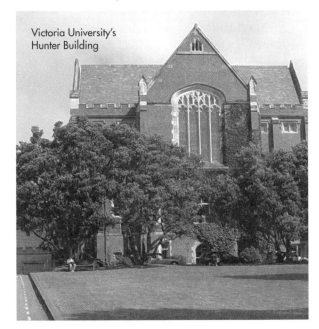

Victoria University's Hunter Building

Even more scary, it took until 1964 for the university to completely remove some six truckloads of radioactive material from the Hunter Building, shifting it to a storage shed in Wai-Te-Ata Road, a residential street beside the graveyard near the Student Union building. Final disposal at the Wilton Road tip took another two years.

Slack safety standards involving the use of radium were apparently the cause of the contamination. There were stories about professors carrying lumps of radium around in their pockets. The office of professor Ernest Marsden, who worked with Ernest Rutherford on splitting the atom, had the highest level of contamination - the ceiling walls, light switches and even the taps were found to be radioactive.

University officials involved in the scare have since admitted a cover-up, saying they didn't want to alarm the public, who only heard that there had been a "small amount" of contamination found on some lab equipment when a newspaper ran a story on the Humphrey legal case. The actual extent of contamination was much worse than they let on.

Victoria University restored the Hunter Building in the early 1990s. It is radiation-free nowadays and contains the offices of the university's top managers. The Wilton Road tip is now the site of a sports field (Ian Galloway Park). The Hunter Building's radioactive waste lies more than seven metres below the grounds - far enough down to avoid health risks (so we're told).

4. Mt Victoria

There's more than hobbits hiding from Nazgul on the slopes of Mt Victoria, which have a bloody and criminal past that rivals some of the city's seedier streets.

Gay men have used secluded areas, especially those on the southern flanks near the old chest hospital, as cruising areas and a place for sexual liaisons for more than 60 years. Stories abound of mountain bikers and walkers on side tracks stumbling across mating scenes 'suitable' for the National Geographic channel.

Louis Chemis, an Italian road worker and convicted murderer, put a stick of dynamite in his mouth and blew his head off on the top of Mt Victoria in 1898. Chemis had been convicted of stabbing a Kaiwharawhara farmer to death with a stiletto knife following a lease dispute in 1889. He was sentenced to death, but had that commuted to life following public disquiet about the case. He was released from prison in

1897 under an amnesty celebrating Queen Victoria's 60th jubilee.

His reputation in tatters and unable to find work, Chemis was inspired by the suicide of MP William Larnach in the parliamentary buildings. Ten days after Larnach's death, boozed on brandy, he climbed Mt Victoria with a stick of dynamite.

Another suicide caused controversy in 1947, mainly because of doubts whether death was self-inflicted. A man fixing his radio aerial found 17-year-old Marie West's decomposing body in the Mt Victoria bush behind her family home in McIntyre Avenue, off Hawker Street ~ some three months after she went missing on her way to Courtenay Place to meet a friend. She had a cut rope twisted around her neck. Pathologists ruled death by strangulation and suspected the body had been cut down from a tree after hanging. There was no sign of her coat, cardigan, shoes and other personal items. The coroner issued an open verdict on what had caused the strangulation.

Louis Chemis

A year later another death on the hill triggered a parliamentary debate and firmed National's resolve to bring back hanging. Some boys found the body of Katherine Cranston, a 47-year-old English widow, down a bank below Alexandra Road near the summit on 26 September 1948. She had been bashed, raped, stabbed and strangled. A young blacksmith, Edward Horton, was found guilty of the murder and sentenced to life imprisonment with hard labour.

5.   Mt Victoria tunnel

A high-profile murder marred the construction of the Mt Victoria tunnel in 1931. Police discovered 17-year-old Phyllis Symons's body buried face down among the tunnel excavations in Hataitai Park. More than 100 officers and relief workers had spent five days digging through the rubble after a report that George Coats ~ Symons's lover ~ had been spotted in

Above: Police and tunnel workers uncovered a grisly secret.
Alexander Turnbull Library G24796 1/1

Right: Opening the Mt Victoria tunnel in 1931.
Alexander Turnbull Library G24651 1/1

the area with a shovel (he claimed he was there to bury a dog). Coats had been employed at the earthworks as a relief worker, and Symons, before disappearing, had stayed with him in his Adelaide Road boarding room after running away from her parents in Brooklyn.

The pathologist ruled that Symons had been bashed in the right temple after being forced to kneel beside a prepared grave. She was hit again when she tried to rise, but was still alive when buried. She was found to be pregnant. Coats was hanged for the murder at Mt Crawford prison on 17 December 1931.

6. Home Street, Mt Victoria

This now undistinguished Mt Victoria street was a favourite for Wellington's criminal underworld in the early 1970s. Dean Wickliffe (*see* Te Aro, No 4) lived there with prostitutes before trying to rob the Royal Oak Jewellers in 1972. He described it "as one of the most notorious streets in the country, and by far the most notorious in Wellington", calling it "a tiny dead-end consisting of a score of houses occupied by criminals, prostitutes, drag queens and every other type of social reject imaginable".

7. 70 Roxburgh Street, Mt Victoria

This house was the scene of the vile murder of a Justice Department clerk in 1986. It was one of Wellington's most vicious killings, and one that places Rufus Marsh, the convicted culprit, near the top of New Zealand's most dangerous criminal list. Marsh was already a convicted killer ~ found guilty of manslaughter in 1975 for helping kick a pensioner to death in Hopper Street (*see* Te Aro, No 20). He was just out of Mt Crawford prison for aggravated robbery at the time of the Mt Victoria murder.

Marsh was seen walking around Mt Victoria on November 20, allegedly casing houses in the area for a victim, using his knowledge of flats into which he had helped move women while working for Shift-A-Flat, a Wellington removal firm. He chose Diane Miller, a 32-year-old living at 70 Roxburgh Street. Marsh slipped into the house through the unlocked back door. Bashing Diane over the head with a paving brick, he dragged her into an upstairs bedroom and tried to rape her before stabbing her repeatedly in the neck with a kitchen knife. Diane's body was found with nick wounds over her face ~ evidence that Marsh had tortured her before cutting her throat and carotid artery.

Her flatmate and a friend returned home to find the flat locked. They rang the doorbell and while walking around the house saw a man running off down the street. Their description was good enough for police to pick up Marsh, found with bloodstained clothes and hands at the bottlestore near the bottom of Majoribanks Street.

Marsh pleaded not guilty, claiming he had met another man he knew (the murderer) coming out of the flat, but that he couldn't name him for fear of retribution. He gave a rambling, aggressive and contradictory defence of himself on the witness stand. The evidence was overwhelmingly against him, but that didn't stop a furious response to the guilty verdict. Marsh yelled at the judge and momentarily overpowered his guards in an attempt to climb out of the dock, screaming, "I'll get you" at the flatmate who had identified him.

Marsh is officially eligible for life parole. It's doubtful he'll be back on the streets any time soon. The psychiatrist who interviewed Marsh to see whether he was fit to stand trial wrote in his report that it was "extremely likely" that he would harm someone in the future if returned to the community.

8. The shooting of Bruce Glensor ~ corner Glenmore Street & Garden Road

Bruce Glensor, 22, was the first person to die from a police bullet since West Coast farmer and cop killer Stanley Graham in 1941. He bled to death on 16 April 1970 after an Armed Offenders Squad member shot him at the intersection of Glenmore Street and Garden Road for waving a shotgun at a police officer. The shooting followed one of the biggest manhunts in Wellington's history.

The drama started the day before when Glensor, a borstal boy, took it too far. Armed with a sawn-off shotgun he kidnapped 17-year-old Julie Campbell from her parents' home in Fernlea Avenue, Karori. He was on the run from police after stealing firearms from Tisdalls sports store a couple of days earlier.

Glensor surprised three detectives in a police car in Collier Avenue later that evening when he jumped down a bank, dragging his hostage with him. He fired a shot into the car's glovebox, demanding that one of the detectives give up his pistol. The detectives dived out of the car and ran for it.

He eluded searchers, who were frantically scouring Karori by hiding out at his Northland house at 23

Garden Road (now 25 Garden Road). From there he called police, allegedly saying he intended to kill the girl. His parents and Julie Campbell's father had gone on 2ZB earlier that evening to implore him to come home, saying the police had assured them he would not be harmed.

The police twigged that Glensor had moved to Northland after a relative rang to say there were lights on at the formerly unoccupied house. The Armed Offenders Squad immediately surrounded the property. At about 10pm Glensor came out of house with the shotgun pointed at two hostages (Julie Campbell and a lodger from the house) and a rifle strapped to his back. Followed by Armed Offended Squad members, they marched down Garden Road then down the steps into Glenmore Street, Julie Campbell crying and shaking with hysteria as they went.

Glensor tried to take a police car blocking the intersection. Finding the keys weren't there, he started to walk down Glenmore Street. A dog handler approached. Glensor turned and pointed the shotgun. Whatever his intention, he didn't get a chance to fire. A squad member pulled his trigger as Campbell screamed, "Don't shoot!"

The shot was only intended to wound Glensor, but instead of hitting his leg, the bullet ripped through Glensor's pelvis and liver. He died on the way to hospital.

6.
Outside Wellington ~ Lower Hutt

No guide to Wellington's dark side would be complete without some mention of Lower Hutt ('Hutt City', to use its newly adopted moniker).

Lower Hutt has the darkest reputation of the Wellington region's four cities. It was known as the murder capital of New Zealand in the 1980s and has regularly topped the national stats for violent crime. In the 1970s it was the scene of brutal gang confrontations between Black Power and the Mongrel Mob (which first formed in Petone).

Sociologists point to the city's enormous wealth disparity as a cause of its appalling crime record. The central city area is home to some of the most affluent people in the country, while the northern suburbs of Naenae and Taita contain the poorest. Whatever the reason, the city has seen some hideous crimes.

1. *"Help, a policeman has been shot"* ~ 7 Herbert Street

A ginger-headed toolmaker shot dead two young police constables with a hunting rifle from the bay window of 7 Herbert Street on 3 February 1963. The shocking killing, following soon after a double shooting of two Auckland policemen, led to the establishment of the police's Armed Offenders Squad.

Constables Bryan Schultz, 22, and James Richardson, 25, pulled up outside the small cottage on the sunny Sunday evening around 5pm. They were responding to a domestic dispute after a call from a distressed woman from a dairy on the corner of Herbert Street and Railway Avenue. The black Holden police car had just come to a halt when three shots rang out from a Lee Enfield .303 rifle. One bullet hit Richardson in the head; another slammed into Schultz's chest. Both died instantly.

A young boy from a neighbouring home alerted the police of the shooting, calling '111' with the message,

7 Herbert Street ~ site of a double police killing.

"Please help, a policeman has been shot." He watched two boarders from the house rush outside and overpower the gunman ~ 27-year-old Bruce McPhee ~ in the driveway. McPhee got a life sentence for the double murder (he was paroled after 11 years), becoming the first person to be convicted for killing a New Zealand police officer.

The death house stands today in immaculate condition near the foot of the Ewen Bridge.

2. Elbe's Milk Bar site, 98 High Street

Elbe's was at the centre of a 1954 sex scandal involving teenage bikers and their underage girlfriends ~ nicknamed bodgies and widgies by the press and Wellington bureaucrats. The resulting public inquiry into adolescent delinquency laid the basis for a

Molotov cocktails (also inset) among the debris from a 1978 gang fight in Waione Street, Petone.
Alexander Turnbull Library Dominion Post collection 1978/37/28/10

conservative backlash by Sid Holland's government against teenage rebellion and the emerging rock'n'roll generation.

The milkbar in lower High Street was a favourite hangout for Wellington motorcycle gangs. The bikers would roar out there in the weekends, sitting outside combing their hair and tooting at girls. Elbe's also provided a meeting place to arrange trysts at nearby Strang Park or down by the Hutt River.

The milkbar cowboys' behaviour incited public

outrage after a report in the *Evening Post* about an 18-year-old Wellington man charged with carnal knowledge of a minor. He had met the 15-year-old (who, shockingly, wore make-up, smoked cigarettes and drank alcohol) at Elbe's. They had gone to the pictures, but left at half-time to have sex at the Petone recreation ground. More salacious court cases followed.

Police responded to the outrage by rounding up 59 teenagers and charging them with some 107 offences. The media had a field day with stories about orgies in homes while parents were absent and other examples of "immoral conduct".

An election beckoning, the government felt forced to act. It set up the Special Committee on Moral Delinquency in Children and Adolescents, chaired by Oswald Mazengarb ~ a puritanical lawyer and close friend of prime minister Sid Holland. The resulting 'Mazengarb Report' largely blamed the problem on slack parental discipline. It also criticised the availability of condoms to teenagers and attacked working mothers and excessive wages for teenagers.

And it singled out teenage "huntresses" for leading the boys astray. A ban on the sale of contraceptives to teenagers under 16 followed. It even became illegal to provide instructions on their use.

The report broadened the definition of 'obscene' and indecent' to include subjects that covered crime, sex and horror ~ a move that provided Jack Marshall, National's justice minister and zealous moral arbiter, with the basis for introducing strict censorship laws. One of the first of the 'filthy' books and comics to go was the Lone Ranger ~ because it was an offence to wear a mask in New Zealand.

A Chinese restaurant and takeaway bar now occupies the site where Elbe's Milk Bar stood in 1954.

3. St Albans Grove, Woburn

The steps leading up to the stopbank walkway at the far end of the leafy grove are where Terence Traynor snatched Kahutaurere Durie ('baby Kahu') ~ the eight-month-old adopted daughter of feisty Maori lawyer Donna Hall and Justice Eddie Durie, chairman of the Waitangi Tribunal.

Traynor, 54, had hoped to get a $3 million ransom, but was foiled when police swooped on his specially prepared hideout eight days later in Taumarunui.

He had initially intended to kidnap Donna Hall after getting her name from a 'rich list' published in the *Sunday-Star Times*, but decided she would be too much to handle. On the morning of 13 April 2002 he watched Hall leave her home with baby Kahu in a pushchair, accompanied by her two nieces and the family dog. Seeing where she was heading, Traynor drove to the end of St Albans Grove and waited outside the Lower Hutt City Childcare Centre.

The nieces arrived first, pushing the pram. Traynor ran out wearing a balaclava and carrying a cut-down .22 Ruger rifle. Pointing the gun, he threatened the girls and ordered them to leave the baby and walk up the steps. Hall, walking behind, was also threatened and told to get rid of the dog. Traynor grabbed the baby and put her in the front seat of his car. Hall ran onto the road to stop him and had to jump out of the way as Traynor sped off.

Four days later the ransom note arrived with polaroid photos of the baby. It demanded $1 million in $100 bills, $1 million in $50 bills and $1 million in gold coins. The note and a phone call to Hall to see if the ransom was ready helped police track Traynor down at Taumarunui.

Traynor had looked after Kahu and she was returned to her parents in good health. He pleaded guilty to kidnapping and other charges on 26 April, earning himself, instead of $3 million, a prison sentence of eleven years.

4.   101 Victoria Street, Alicetown

Ernie Engelbrecht, an elderly and eccentric pensioner, bought the house at the corner of Victoria Street and Te Mome Road to woo a German war widow.

She never got to see the house, falling instead for a Murchison goldminer who, like Engelbrecht, had answered her newspaper ad. Instead of a love nest, the house became a murder site when the 94-year-old was brutally bashed to death in his bed in July 1979 ~ a murder that has never been solved.

Engelbrecht, himself a German immigrant, was well known in area as 'the old man' and for pushing a small cart around building sites scavenging for firewood.

Police were convinced the killer lived locally, and may have been one of the old man's many casual visitors

Meant to be a love nest, this house at the corner of Victoria Street and Te Mome Road became a murder site.

5. Slaying of the Joneses ~ corner Jackson & Beach Streets, Petone

Etienne Brocher, a former convict who had served in the French Foreign Legion, stabbed to death the elderly owners of a grocery store on this corner on 27 August 1896. The crime was one of the most shocking in Petone's history. Miscreant children today are still warned to be wary of the evil Frenchman's ghost.

Brocher first blinded the shopkeepers (Joseph and Emma Jones) by throwing white pepper in their eyes, then made off with their cashbox. Suspicion initially

who bludged a meal or a bed for the night. The massive inquiry included a swoop on the pubs in the area to check fingerprints of drinkers against a print found at the house. Police examined 2500 prints but didn't find a match.

The shop at the front of the property that Engelbrecht intended to be a photographic studio for his new bride is now a hair salon.

Beware the ghost of the knife-crazed French Foreign Legionnaire.

Hutt Park Hotel in Randwick Road

fell on a local drunk, a one-time boner for the Gear Meat Company. Brocher was serving two years' hard labour at The Terrace Gaol for bigamy when police finally decided to charge him for the murders. He pleaded innocent, but was convicted and sentenced to death. He finally confessed before being hanged at the prison on 21 April 1897 (*see* Other infamous city sites, No 2).

The grocer's shop and murder site was based where the TAB and Petone Sports Bar now stands. It's thought that a section of the original murder house was relocated to 34 Bay Street, to become part of a doctor's surgery. It is now a boarding house.

6.   Hutt Park Hotel, 9-11 Randwick Road

The Hutt Park Hotel was a violent Black Power haunt in the early 1980s. There were calls, most notably from then MP, later Lower Hutt mayor, John Terris, to close the pub down in the wake of the Paul Chase shooting in 1983 (*see* No 7).

7.   Menkar Apartments ~ 447 Jackson Street, Petone

An Armed Offenders Squad bullet killed Mongrel Mob associate Paul Chase after an early morning raid on the Housing Corporation flats (across the road from Unilever's glass offices) on 18 April 1983.

Following only a few months after the John Morgan shooting (*see* Te Aro, No 7), the killing attracted angry condemnation of seemingly trigger-happy New Zealand cops. Like Morgan, Chase wasn't carrying a gun.

The police raid followed a fight during the weekend at the nearby Hutt Park Hotel in Randwick Road (*see* No 6) in which someone in Chase's party had fired a shotgun into the ceiling. Police cordoned off the apartment building before moving in just after 6.30am,

Menkar Apartments

to the silver-barrelled shotgun from the pub fight. They were later cleared by a independent inquiry that concluded they had acted within policy guidelines, but recommended a reappraisal of some Armed Offenders Squad practices (changes were announced in May 1984).

Justified or not, there was widespread criticism of the shooting. The outcry from Wellington Maori leaders was among the most vociferous. There were rumours that the Mongrel Mob was planning the revenge killing of a cop. Prime minister Rob Muldoon didn't help ease the tension by commenting, "If I had been the policeman, I would have shot him".

climbing up the stairs to Chase's flat~ one of the top rear units (No 35) in the three-storey apartment block. After getting no response to a knock, they jemmied the door open and rushed in.

Chase, whose wife and child were in an adjacent room, came around the corner of the hallway carrying an exercise bar. A squad member fired a .357 revolver, hitting him in the stomach. He died later that morning, despite surgery at Hutt Hospital.

The police argued the bar appeared strikingly similar

8.   207 Waterloo Road

The brutal clubbing of businessman Robert Cancian at his 207 Waterloo Road home in 1983 unearthed an ugly side of Lower Hutt ~ its criminal underworld.

Two men, armed with a softball bat and a sawn-off shotgun, pushed their way into Cancian's home about 10.15pm on 25 February 1983. They bound him to the bed with tape and forced his girlfriend and her mother to the floor. Just before leaving, after grabbing money and jewellery, the man with the bat clubbed Cancian several times on the back of his head. He died from his injuries several days later.

The police used information from underworld contacts to arrest Wayne Carstairs and Michael Sneller. Two of the informants were never identified during the trial ~ the first use of the Witness Protection Scheme in New Zealand. The Crown argued the defendants had been hired to seek retribution for a failed business deal. Carstairs and Sneller were both found guilty of murder, although no one was ever charged with contracting them.

Sneller also had connections with another suspected incident of underworld skulduggery ~ one that attracted widespread media interest in 1980. He was the de facto husband of Marion Granville, who disappeared on 30 August 1980 after leaving her home in Wilkie Crescent, Naenae to get cigarettes from a dairy in Seddon Street. A witness saw her talking to a man outside her car before being dragged into a white Holden. Her car was mysteriously returned to her home two hours after her disappearance. She and Sneller were due to appear in court two days later on charges of possessing cannabis for supply. The rumour was that someone wanted her silenced.

9.   Death of a bank teller, Naenae Trust Bank branch site, 25 Everest Avenue

A fried chicken takeaway now occupies the former location of the Naenae Trust Bank. Bank teller Bill Brown had his brains spilled by a shotgun blast while trying to stop a robbery in the building on 29 January 1997.

The robber, 19-year-old Anton Matenga, had just finished a short stint at Rimutaka prison that morning. Picked up at the prison gates by a Mongrel Mob prospect, he had been given instructions, a sawn-off shotgun and an electronic pager so he could be alerted if anything went wrong. The shotgun was visible in his bag as he walked around the Hillary Court shopping complex on his way to the bank just before 10am. He had a balaclava and a stocking on his head, but forgot to pull them down when he entered the bank.

Alerted by his pager that the police were on their way from the Naenae station (just 200m up the road), Matenga herded tellers and customers into a back room. Scared and panicky, he let four of the hostages go with notes for his family and a demand that the police bring his girlfriend to the bank.

Down to just three hostages, he was standing in

a narrow hallway looking distractedly out the back of the bank when 49-year-old Bill Brown leapt from the staff tearooms in an attempt to disarm him. The almost point blank blast caught Brown midair in a flying tackle, taking the top of his head off.

Matenga dropped the gun and walked out with his arms raised. Covered in Brown's blood and brain tissue, he surrendered to police, calling, "Don't shoot, don't shoot, I've just got out of Rimutaka!"

Matenga was duly convicted of murder, receiving a life sentence. Chris Lemalie ~ the Mongrel Mob prospect who picked up Matenga on the morning of the robbery ~ also got life for murder. Two others were found guilty of manslaughter for their part in 'masterminding' the hold-up ~ Mongrel Mob chapter head Mark Mahaki and his de facto wife Roseanne Te Moni. Mahaki sourced the shotgun and ammunition used in the robbery. Te Moni's role was to monitor police communications. She kept contact with Lemalie who stayed near the bank while Matenga was inside, and was the one who used the pager to alert Matenga that the police were on their way.

The branch never reopened. WestpacTrust announced in February 1997 it couldn't ask staff to work at the building again and that it would merge the Naenae operation with its Lower Hutt office.

10. Taita's horror house ~ 54 Churton Crescent

The two-storey Housing Corporation house at 54 Churton Crescent oozes evil. It is where Paul Dally tortured and raped 13-year-old Karla Cardno, holding her captive before bashing her face in with a lump of wood near the Pencarrow sewer outfall in 1989.

It was a sickening crime, one that local police rate as the most horrific in living memory.

Dally, a 28-year-old sewer pipe cleaner, had lived alone at the property since his de facto wife walked out on him with their three kids a month before the killing. On 26 May, a cold and blustery Friday evening, he snatched Karla from the corner of Churton Crescent and Taine Street when she stopped to rearrange her shopping while biking home (to 26 Churton Crescent) from the Taita shopping centre.

Dally pulled her into some bushes, then dragged her through the neighbouring front yards back to 54 Churton Crescent, where he gagged and bound her to a bed in an upstairs room before raping her. The room looks out onto the street. Dally would have seen Karla's family searching and calling for her when she failed to return home. He kept her in that room for more than 20 hours, before locking her, gagged with masked tape and naked, into the boot of his Valiant and driving to Pencarrow Head. Karla probably watched as he dug the grave and selected a nearby log to club her to death.

Dally led police to the beachfront grave some six weeks later. He had confessed to the crime after mounting evidence, including strands of Karla's hair and fibre from her clothing in the fireplace at 54 Churton Crescent and in a vacuum cleaner he had borrowed from the Hutt Valley Drainage Board (his employer). He was sentenced to life imprisonment in March 1990 and is now eligible for parole.

11. Matiu/Somes Island

This island in Wellington harbour is shrouded with dark secrets. It has harboured cannibals, suspected lepers and Nazis. And for the enemy aliens interned there during the first and second world wars, it was Wellington's very own Alcatraz.

Let's start with its former Maori occupants… The island was the base from which Ngati Mutunga launched their invasion of the Chatham Islands in 1835. They and their Taranaki cousins, Ngati Tama, seized the brig *Rodney* and forced (or bribed) the captain to ship their warriors to the islands, where they slaughtered and devoured nearly one fifth of the unresisting native Moriori population.

In the early 1870s, following a smallpox scare aboard an immigrant ship, the island became a quarantine station. In 1903 the authorities quarantined Kim Lee, an immigrant from Canton. Following a tip-off, police tracked him down at a Newtown fruitshop. He was found to have enlarged glands, a suppurating bubo in his groin and psoriasis on much of his body. Fearful of the dreaded disease, the island's other inhabitants didn't welcome his arrival. He was soon banished to a small islet just north of Somes, Nga Mokopuna, sometimes called Leper Island.

Lee died a few months after arrival and was buried in an unmarked grave. Later examination of his medical records suggested he may not have had leprosy, but tuberculosis or an immunity deficiency. Some believe his isolation was more the result of racism than disease.

The island served as an internment camp for enemy aliens during the first and second world wars.

World War I prisoners on the march on Matiu (Somes Island), to the strains of violin and accordion.
Alexander Turnbull Library F75448 1/2

Allegations of internee mistreatment during World War I, including beatings and forced labour, led to a judicial inquiry in 1918. Major Dugald Matheson, the hated camp commander, was the target of many of the allegations. Internees regarded him as incompetent, a drunk and a brute. The inquiry cleared Matheson, but accepted that, contravening the Hague convention, internees had been forced to perform gruelling labour.

Somes became an internment camp again in 1939. A shortage of accommodation forced German Jews and socialists to bunk beside fanatical Nazis ~ a move that hardly led to harmonious relations among internees. Hardcore Nazis openly paraded their support of Hitler during the early years of the war, wearing cardboard swastikas and celebrating the Führer's birthday. That support waned somewhat during the war's latter years, and by 1945 hardly anyone was admitting to be pro-Nazi.

And stranger than science fiction… the island had a role in the secret development of a ray gun by a Takapuna motor mechanic. Victor Penny came to the attention of military authorities in 1935 when he claimed a foreign power had offered him money to develop a weapon that used radio waves to knock out enemy aircraft. A keen radio buff, Penny had apparently already created a transmitter that could ignite a box of matches. The government set him up with a laboratory to continue his experiments in the old hospital building on Somes. He was given armed guards, who had orders to shoot intruders. Lack of results saw the government abandon the project six months later and send Penny ('Mr Smith') home.

Some useful references

Avanti, Micheal *Twisted Soul*, PSL Press, Wellington 1999

Bungay, Mike & Brian Edwards *Bungay on Murder*, Whitcoulls 1983

Carmen (Trevor Rupe) *Carmen, My Life*, Benton Ross 1988

Jordan, Jan *Working Girls: Women in the New Zealand Sex Industry Talk to Jan Jordan*, Penguin Books 1991

Maysmor, Bob *By His Excellency's Command: the Adventurous Life of David Stark Durie* Puka Press Porirua 2002

McGill, David *A Capital Century*, Transpress 2003
— *Island of Secrets*, Steele Roberts in association with Silver Owl Press 2001

McLean, Gavin *Wellington, The First Years of European Settlement, 1840-1850*, Penguin Books 2000

Temple, Philip *A Sort of Conscience: The Wakefields* Auckland University Press 2002

Williams, Tony *A Case of Murder: Bizarre and Unsolved Murders in New Zealand*, Hodder Moa Beckett 2000
— *The A-Z of the Bad, the Very Bad and the Ugly: Who's Who of NZ Crime*, Hodder Moa Beckett 1998

Young, Sherwood (ed) *With Confidence and Pride, Policing the Wellington Region, 1840-1992*, Wellington Police Trust 1994

Yska, Redmer *All Shook Up, The Flash Bodgie and the Rise of the New Zealand Teenager in the Fifties*, Penguin Books 1993

Index